First World War
and Army of Occupation
War Diary
France, Belgium and Germany

48 DIVISION
Divisional Troops
240 South Midland Brigade Royal Field Artillery
1 March 1915 - 31 October 1917

WO95/2749/3

The Naval & Military Press Ltd
www.nmarchive.com
Published in association with The National Archives

Published by

The Naval & Military Press Ltd

Unit 10 Ridgewood Industrial Park,

Uckfield, East Sussex,

TN22 5QE England

Tel: +44 (0) 1825 749494

www.naval-military-press.com

www.nmarchive.com

This diary has been reprinted in facsimile from the original. Any imperfections are inevitably reproduced and the quality may fall short of modern type and cartographic standards.

© **Crown Copyright**
Images reproduced by permission of The National Archives, London, England, 2015.

Contents

Document type	Place/Title	Date From	Date To
Heading	WO95/2749/3 240 South Midland Bde RFA Mar 1915-Oct 1917		
Heading	48th Division BEF 1st Sth Mid'd Bde RFA Became 240th S.M. Bde RFA Mar 1915 Oct 1917		
Heading	1st S.M Bde RFA Vol I 1-31.3.15 Mar 19 240 S.M. Bde RFA		
Heading	War Diary Of 1st South Midland Brigade R.F.A. Volume VIII		
War Diary	Broomfield	01/03/1915	29/03/1915
War Diary	Southampton	29/03/1915	29/03/1915
War Diary	Havre	30/03/1915	31/03/1915
Heading	1st S.M. Bde R.F.A. Vol II 1-30.4.15		
Heading	War Diary Of 1st South Midland Brigade RFA From 1/4/15 To 30/4/15 Volume IX		
War Diary	Rouge Croix	01/04/1915	01/04/1915
War Diary	Neuve Eglise	02/04/1915	30/04/1915
Heading	48th Division 1st S.M Bde RFA Vol III 1-31.5.15		
Heading	War Diary Of 1st South Midland Brigade RFA From 1/5/15 To 31/5/15 Volume X		
War Diary	Neuve Eglise	01/05/1915	31/05/1915
Heading	48th Division 1st S.M Bde RFA Vol IV 1-30.6.15		
Heading	War Diary Of 1st South Midland Brigade RFA From 1st June 1915 To 30th June 1915 Volume XI		
War Diary	Neuve Eglise	01/06/1915	26/06/1915
War Diary	Outtersteene	27/06/1915	27/06/1915
War Diary	Vieux Berquin	28/06/1915	28/06/1915
War Diary	Robecq	29/06/1915	29/06/1915
War Diary	Ferfay	30/06/1915	30/06/1915
Heading	48th Division 1st S.M Bde RFA Vol V 1-31-7-15		
Heading	War Diary Of 1st South Midland Brigade RFA From 1st July 1915 To 31st July 1915 (Volume XII)		
War Diary	Ferfay	01/07/1915	19/07/1915
War Diary	Lillers	20/07/1915	20/07/1915
War Diary	Mondicourt	20/07/1915	21/07/1915
War Diary	Thievres	21/07/1915	30/07/1915
War Diary	Sailly	31/07/1915	31/07/1915
Heading	48th Division War Diary Of 1st South Midland Brigade RFA From 1st August To 31st August 1915 Volume VI		
War Diary	Colincamps	01/08/1915	31/08/1915
Heading	War Diary Of 1st South Midland Brigade RFA From September 1st To September 30th 1915 Volume VII		
War Diary	Colincamps	01/09/1915	03/09/1915
War Diary	Hebuterne	03/09/1915	30/09/1915
Heading	War Diary Of 1st South Midland Brigade RFA From Oct 1st To Oct 31st 1915 Vol VIII		
War Diary	Hebuterne	01/10/1915	31/10/1915
Heading	War Diary Of 1st South Midland Brigade RFA From Nov 1st To Nov 30th 1915 Volume IX		
War Diary	Hebuterne	01/11/1915	30/11/1915

Heading	War Diary Of 1st South Midland Brigade RFA From Dec 1st To Dec 31st 1915 Volume X		
War Diary	Hebuterne	01/12/1915	31/12/1915
Heading	War Diary Of 1st South Midland Brigade RFA From Jan 1st To Jan 31st 1916 Volume XI		
War Diary	Hebuterne	01/01/1916	31/01/1916
Heading	War Diary Of 1st South Midland Brigade RFA From Feb 1st To Feb 29th 1916 Volume XII		
War Diary	Hebuterne	01/02/1916	29/02/1916
Heading	War Diary Of 1/1st South Midland Brigade RFA From March 1st To March 31st 1916 Volume XX		
War Diary	Hebuterne	01/03/1916	14/03/1916
War Diary	Colincamps	15/03/1916	31/03/1916
Heading	War Diary Of 1/1st South Midland Brigade R.F.A. From 1st April To 30th April 1916 Volume XXI		
War Diary	Colincamps	01/04/1916	06/04/1916
War Diary	Sailly	06/04/1916	30/04/1916
Heading	War Diary Of 240th (S. Mid) Brigade RFA From May 1st To May 31st 1916 Volume XXII		
War Diary	Sailly	01/05/1916	31/05/1916
Heading	War Diary Of 240th (S.M) Brigade RFA For June 1916		
War Diary	Sailly	01/06/1916	05/06/1916
War Diary	Coigneux	06/06/1916	17/06/1916
War Diary	Sailly	18/06/1916	30/06/1916
Heading	War Diary Headquarters 240th Brigade R.F.A. July 1916		
Heading	War Diary Of 240th (S.M) Brigade RFA For Period 1st July To 31st July 1916		
War Diary	Sailly	01/07/1916	11/07/1916
War Diary	Coigneux	12/07/1916	20/07/1916
War Diary	Aveluy	21/07/1916	28/07/1916
War Diary	Amplier	29/07/1916	31/07/1916
Heading	48th Divisional Artillery 240th (South Midland) Brigade Royal Field Artillery August 1916		
Heading	War Diary Of 240th (S.M) Brigade RFA For Period 1st Aug To 31st Aug 1916		
War Diary	St Ouen	01/08/1916	09/08/1916
War Diary	Amplier	10/08/1916	12/08/1916
War Diary	Bouzincourt	13/08/1916	27/08/1916
War Diary	Aveluy Wood	28/08/1916	31/08/1916
Heading	48th Divisional Artillery 240th Brigade RFA September 1916		
Heading	War Diary Of 240th (S.M.) Brigade RFA For Period 1st Sept To 30th Sept 1916		
War Diary	Mesnil	01/09/1916	05/09/1916
War Diary	Bouzincourt	06/09/1916	15/09/1916
War Diary	Ovillers	16/09/1916	30/09/1916
Heading	War Diary Of 240th (S.M.) Brigade RFA October 1916		
War Diary	Albert	01/10/1916	02/10/1916
War Diary	Warlincourt	03/10/1916	07/10/1916
War Diary	Souastre	08/10/1916	31/10/1916
Heading	War Diary Of 240th (S.M.) Brigade RFA For The Period 1st November 1916 To 30th November 1916		
War Diary	Souastre	01/11/1916	26/11/1916
War Diary	Pas	27/11/1916	30/11/1916

Heading	War Diary Of 240th (S.M.) Brigade R.F.A. For The Period 1st December 1916 To 31st December 1916 Volume 21		
War Diary	Talmas	01/12/1916	01/12/1916
War Diary	Behencourt	02/12/1916	05/12/1916
War Diary	Bazantin Le Petit	06/12/1916	31/12/1916
Heading	War Diary For The Period 1st January To 31st January 1917 Volume 22 240th (S.M.) Brigade R.F.A.		
War Diary	Behencourt	01/01/1917	13/01/1917
War Diary	Contalmaison Villa	14/01/1917	22/01/1917
War Diary	Bavlincourt	23/01/1917	26/01/1917
War Diary	Fouilloy	27/01/1917	31/01/1917
Heading	War Diary Of 240th (S.M.) Brigade R.F.A. For The Period 1st To 28th February 1917 Volume 24		
War Diary	Fouilloy	01/02/1917	02/02/1917
War Diary	Cappy	03/02/1917	04/02/1917
War Diary	Flaucourt	05/02/1917	28/02/1917
Heading	War Diary Of 240th (S.M.) Brigade R.F.A. For The Period 1st To 31st March 1917 Volume 25		
War Diary	Flaucourt	01/03/1917	22/03/1917
War Diary	Doignt	23/03/1917	23/03/1917
War Diary	Courcelles	24/03/1917	28/03/1917
War Diary	Tincourt	29/03/1917	31/03/1917
Heading	War Diary Of The 240th (S.M.) Brigade R.F.A. For The Period 1st To 30th April 1917		
Miscellaneous	HQ 48th D.A	01/05/1917	01/05/1917
War Diary	Saulcourt Wood	01/04/1917	06/04/1917
War Diary	St Emilie	07/04/1917	30/04/1917
Heading	War Diary Of The 240th (S.M.) Bde R.F.A. For The Period 1st May 1917 To 31st May 1917 Volume 25		
War Diary	St Emilie	01/05/1917	02/05/1917
War Diary	Marquaix	03/05/1917	16/05/1917
War Diary	Beaulencourt	17/05/1917	19/05/1917
War Diary	Beaumetz	20/05/1917	31/05/1917
Heading	War Diary Of The 240th (S.M.) Brigade R.F.A. For The Period 1st June 1917 To 30th June 1917 Volume 27		
War Diary	Beaumetz	01/06/1917	23/06/1917
War Diary	Montauban	24/06/1917	30/06/1917
Heading	War Diary Of The 240th (S.M.) Brigade R.F.A. For The Period 1st To 31st October 1917 Volume 31		
Miscellaneous	Headquarters 48th Div Arty	01/11/1917	01/11/1917
War Diary	Ochtezeele	01/10/1917	04/10/1917
War Diary	Wattou	05/10/1917	06/10/1917
War Diary	Ypres	07/10/1917	13/10/1917
War Diary	Eecke	14/10/1917	14/10/1917
War Diary	Morbecque	15/10/1917	15/10/1917
War Diary	Gonnehem	16/10/1917	16/10/1917
War Diary	Ablain St Nazaire	17/10/1917	18/10/1917
War Diary	Vimy	19/10/1917	27/10/1917
War Diary	Thelus	28/10/1917	31/10/1917

WO 95/2749/3

240 South Midland RDE
RFA

MAR 1915 — OCT 1917

48TH DIVISION

BEF

1ST STH MID'D BDE RFA
BECAME:-
240TH S.M. BDE RFA.
MAR 1915 - ~~MAR 1919~~

Oct 1917

TO ITALY

1st S.M. Bde: R.+A.

Vol I 1-31-3-15

240 S.M. Bde RJA

CONFIDENTIAL

War Diary
of
1st South Midland Brigade R.F.A.

From 1/3/15 to 31/3/15

Volume VIII

[signature] LT. COLONEL,
COMMANDING,
1/1st S. MIDLAND F.A. BRIGADE.

Army Form C. 2118.

WAR DIARY
INTELLIGENCE SUMMARY.
(Erase heading not required.)

Instructions regarding War Diaries and Intelligence Summaries are contained in F.S. Regs., Part II. and the Staff Manual respectively. Title pages will be prepared in manuscript.

Hour, Date, Place		Summary of Events and Information	Remarks and references to Appendices
BROOMFIELD	1st Mar/15 9am	Usual Parades. Musketry.	J/S.
	2nd Mar/15 9am	Usual Parades. Musketry.	
	5.15pm	Officers lecture at CHELMSFORD by Officers returned from FRANCE.	
	7pm	The "Alarm" given to the Brigade. The Units reported "Ready":- 3rd Battery at 6pm. 1st & 2nd " 6.30pm. Amm. Column " 8.50pm. After inspection by OC., Units were dismissed. The Brigade was re-armed with Rifles for Mk VII Ammunition. 68 of the old ones sent to 2/1st Bde, remainder to WEEDON.	J/S.
	3rd Mar/15 9am	Wet morning. Service Lectures. Musketry.	
	afternoon	Reconnaissance of Positions & Brigade & Battery Staffs	
	6.30pm	Occupation of Positions previously selected by S.O.	J/S.
	4th Mar/15 9.15am	Brigade Parade & Route march via GT WALTHAM, PLESHEY, & MASHBURY. Total 16 miles. Returned to billets.	J/S.
	2pm		
	5th Mar/15 9am	Usual Parades. Exam of signallers by Adjutant. Musketry.	J/S.
	6pm	Lecture to Officers by Adjutant.	
	6th Mar/15 9am	Usual Parades. Inspections. Musketry. 9 hours S.A.A. Practice ammunition arrived. CAPT J.B. KELLAR left for Aeroplane Course at SALISBURY.	J/S.

Forms/C.2118/10

Army Form C. 2118.

WAR DIARY
or
INTELLIGENCE SUMMARY.
(Erase heading not required.)

Instructions regarding War Diaries and Intelligence
Summaries are contained in F.S. Regs., Part II.
and the Staff Manual respectively. Title pages
will be prepared in manuscript.

Hour, Date, Place		Summary of Events and Information	Remarks and references to Appendices
BROOMFIELD	7th Mar/15 9 am	Usual parades. Captains & Subalterns Exam paper.	S/B
	8 Mar/15 9.30 am	All units musketry at BOREHAM. Strong wind from the Right accompanied by short sharp snow storms. Light good & results seemed satisfactory. Only completed 3½ practices.	
	Afternoon	Exercise Lectures etc.	S/B
	9 Mar/15 9.30 am	200 men of all Units musketry at BOREHAM, Light good. Light wind from right. Completed all 5 practices. Results satisfactory.	
	Afternoon	Exercise Gun Drill etc. from 5th Tm. Shorthand	
		Extract from London Gazette:- W.F. RIDLER to be 2nd Lieut. 6-3-15 W.H. LANHAM to be 2nd Lieut dy 7-3-15	S/B
	10th Mar/15 9.30 am	200 men musketry at BOREHAM. Light fair only. Results satisfactory. All 5 practices completed.	
	Afternoon	Exercise Signalling, Telephony etc.	
	2 pm	Examination of 1/2 men in Field aid. 9 passed well. 3 failed.	
	6.30 pm	Practice Alarm. Units ordered to occupy positions indicated on a sketch map issued with the orders. Telephone communication between batteries & F.O.O's. Batteries reported ready to fire as follows:- 1/3rd Battery 9.55 pm; 1/1 at Battery 10.30 pm; 1/2nd Battery at 10.35 pm Amn. Column at 10.10 pm. Units reached their Billets between 12 m & 1 am. A very useful evening. Units found their positions by the map well. Telephones worked fairly well but half the value of it is lost through having no Telephone Wagon. The lack of it interferes very seriously with training.	

Army Form C. 2118.

WAR DIARY
INTELLIGENCE SUMMARY.
(Erase heading not required.)

Instructions regarding War Diaries and Intelligence Summaries are contained in F.S. Regs., Part II. and the Staff Manual respectively. Title pages will be prepared in manuscript.

Hour, Date, Place	Summary of Events and Information	Remarks and references to Appendices
BROOMFIELD 10th Mar/15.	MAJ. C.W. TODD returned from FRANCE.	L/B
11th Mar/15.	Normal parades.	L/B
5 pm	Lecture by MAJ. TODD to all officers. Brig-General Emly R.A. was present.	
12th Mar/15 9 am.	The Brigade proceeded to HOWE STREET & occupied billets in Shelleton. Afterwards proceeded to occupy positions after which they returned to their billets where dinners had been cooked & the Brigade returned home about 3.30 p.m. A very instructive day on the lines of Pt III Notes from the Front. 40 men arrived from 2/1st Bde. LIEUT H.P. LANE returned from course at WOOLWICH.	L/B
13th Mar/15 9am.	Usual parades & inspections. Instruction in Hello by Adjutant. 41 men arrived from NORTHAMPTON from 2/1st Bde to complete 4 for Div. Amm. Park.	L/B
14th Mar/15 11 am.	Church Parade. Open air service. Telephone test. CAPT J.B. KELLAR returned from aeroplane course at SALISBURY.	L/B
15th Mar/15 9 am.	Usual parades. Musketry cancelled.	L/B
16th Mar/15 9 am.	Usual Parades. 23 men left to join Div. Amm. Park. 21 men unfit left to join 2/1st Bde & 29 men arrived from 2/1st Bde. All leave stopped.	L/B
17th Mar/15 9 am.	Usual Parades. Night Alarm. Batteries turned out & occupied (in sheltered) positions in accordance with orders issued at 7 p.m. The vehicles did a Route march & the whole returned to billets at 10.40 p.m.	L/B

Army Form C. 2118.

WAR DIARY
of
INTELLIGENCE SUMMARY.
(Erase heading not required.)

Instructions regarding War Diaries and Intelligence Summaries are contained in F.S. Regs., Part II. and the Staff Manual respectively. Title pages will be prepared in manuscript.

Hour, Date, Place	Summary of Events and Information	Remarks and references to Appendices
BROOMFIELD 18th Mar/15 9am	Usual Parade. The work is almost entirely administrative in connection with the arrival of stores & preparing to leave. Extracts from LONDON Gazette :- W.F. RIDLER from 5th Glou: Regt. to be 2nd Lieut d/- 6th March. J.W.H. LANHAM to be 2nd Lieut d/- 7th March.	G/S
19th Mar/15 9.15am	Heavy fall of snow during night. Inspection of all horses of the Brigade by Major HAMBRO DADR. Exercise complete.	
2 pm	Supply of March VII SAA arrived during afternoon, all battery.	
5 pm	Harness arrived also. Other stores arrived during the day. 2 Lieut F ELLERTON left for temporary duty with Div A.C.	E/B
20th Mar/15 8.45am	Headquarters + Ammunition Column harness arrived. Stores continually arriving all day. Issuing, greasing etc harness	E/B
10 pm	Maj: DUNSCOMBE + 2 O.R. arrived to take over.	E/B
21st Mar/15	Harness fitting, greasing etc. General administrative work. 2 S + D horses received. 2nd Lieut. LINDREA + 2 O.R. arrived to take over. More stores arrived during the day.	E/B
22nd Mar/15	Administrative work. All MkVI S.A.A. despatched to WOOLWICH 8 horses left for LEAMINGTON Vet. Hospital. Harness now complete throughout also Vehicles. Route march (the first) by Ammunition Column with new Harness & Vehicles.	G/S

Army Form C. 2118.

WAR DIARY
INTELLIGENCE SUMMARY.
(Erase heading not required.)

Instructions regarding War Diaries and Intelligence Summaries are contained in F.S. Regs., Part II. and the Staff Manual respectively. Title pages will be prepared in manuscript.

Hour, Date, Place	Summary of Events and Information	Remarks and references to Appendices
BROOMFIELD 23rd Mar/15 9am	CAPT PRIDAY left for embarkation overseas for "Landing duties". Packing of Vehicles, fitting of harness, route marches, etc.	
5.30pm	22 Reinforcements received. Lecture to officers by the Sanitary officer of the Division.	2/S
24th Mar/15	As for 23rd "	2/S
25th Mar/15	Route Marches. Packing trials & usual parades.	4/S
26th Mar/15	As for 25th. Stores coming in slowly each day.	2/S
6 pm	CAPT: FARRELL A.V.C. arrived to take Veterinary charge of the Brigade vice CAPT CADE.	2/S
27th Mar/15 9 am	Route marches etc.	
11.30 am	Time Table of move received as follows:- Amm Col: 2.35 & 4.35 pm. 25th; 1st Bty 10.35 pm. 28th & 12.35 am. 29th; 2nd Battery 4.10 am & 6.10 am. 29th; 3rd Battery 6.10 am & 10.40 am. 29th.	
	CAPT CADE left for BURY ST EDMUNDS on joining 1/1st East Anglian Division.	4/S
28th Mar/15	Day spent in final arrangements.	
3 pm	Amm Column left for train which was altered to 6.35 & 8.35 pm.	
10 pm	Headquarters & 2nd/½ of 1st Battery left BROOMFIELD & entrained at CHELMSFORD. One horse very troublesome & departure delayed 15 mins in consequence.	2/S
29th Mar/15 12.50 am	Left CHELMSFORD. The 2nd & 3rd Batteries entrained at WITHAM	2/S

Army Form C. 2118.

WAR DIARY
or
INTELLIGENCE SUMMARY.
(Erase heading not required.)

Instructions regarding War Diaries and Intelligence Summaries are contained in F.S. Regs., Part II. and the Staff Manual respectively. Title pages will be prepared in manuscript.

Hour, Date, Place		Summary of Events and Information	Remarks and references to Appendices
SOUTHAMPTON	6.30 a.m. 29th Mar/15 7.10 p.m.	Arrived SOUTHAMPTON & embarked on CITY OF LUCKNOW and HUANCHACO. Left on HUANCHACO. Splendid passage no casualties in brigade. The brigade was distributed among 25 ships in some cases one complete unit in a ship.	S/B
HAVRE 30th	5.30 p.m.	Arrived HAVRE. Disembarked & watered & fed all brigade horses on HALLE 3	S/B
	2 p.m. 4 p.m. 9 p.m.	Drew stores etc to complete. L. MIGNO & 7th Siege Arty joined as Interpreters. Paraded & marched to station to entrain. Headquarters train with 1st Battery left HAVRE.	
31st	10.15 a.m. 10.50 a.m. 6 p.m. 9.30 p.m.	Arrived ABBEVILLE. Horses watered & fed. Breakfasts. Left ABBEVILLE (LT LANE & FULLERTON nearly left behind.) Arrived HAZEBRUCK & began detraining at 7.15 p.m. after which we marched 1½ miles to billets at ROUGE CROIX 2 miles SE of CAESTRE. The Units arrived as follows: 1st Battery 11.30 p.m. 2nd Bty 9.15 p.m. 3rd Bty 7 p.m. Amm Col. 1.30 a.m. on 1st.	S/B

Aud Balfour
LT. COLONEL,
COMMANDING,
1/1st S. MIDLAND F.A. BRIGADE.

121/5194

1st S.M. Bde R.F.A.

Vol II 1 – 30.4.15

CONFIDENTIAL.

War Diary

of

1st South Midland Brigade R.F.A.

from 1/4/15 to 30/4/15

Volume IX.

[signature]
LT. COLONEL,
COMMANDING,
1/1st S. MIDLAND F.A. BRIGADE.

Army Form C. 2118.

WAR DIARY
or
INTELLIGENCE SUMMARY.
(Erase heading not required.)

Instructions regarding War Diaries and Intelligence Summaries are contained in F.S. Regs., Part II. and the Staff Manual respectively. Title pages will be prepared in manuscript.

Hour, Date, Place		Summary of Events and Information	Remarks and references to Appendices
ROUGE CROIX 1st April/15			
	8 pm.	The morning was spent in inspecting horses, harness cleaning & completing sanitary arrangements. C.O., Adjutant, orderly officer & 3 O.R. of Headquarters, and 3 officers & 5 O.R. per battery left in 2 motor buses for attachment to 27th Brigade N.A.	
	11 pm.	Arrived NIEPPE and reported to 4th Div. Artillery H.Q.	S/b
	1.30 pm.	arrived NEUVE EGLISE. 1st battery attached to 121st Bty, 2nd to 120th and 3rd to 119th Bty. 27th Brigade belongs to 5th Div. but is lent to 4th Div.	
	5.15 pm.	Visited positions	
NEUVE EGLISE 2nd April	8.30 am.	Visited H.Q., R.A. 5th Div. & 4th Div. & returned to select positions & observing stations for the brigade. The day was spent at this. Two subalterns 2nd battery spent the day with F.O.O.	S/b
3rd April	9.30 am.	LE ROSSIGNOLD Preparation of selected positions. A subaltern of 3rd Bty with F.O.O.	S/b
4th April	2.30 pm.	Inspection of positions by Brig.-Gen. FOX and BUTLER.	S/b
	5 pm.	2nd battery arrived from ROUGE CROIX & proceeded to occupy the prepared positions	S/b
	7 pm.		
5th April	9 am.	Reconnaissance of positions in rear.	
	11.30 am.	2nd Bty registered Registers 1, 2, 3, 4, 4.5, & are allotted sectors A (Reg. 1-3) i.e. from PETITE DOUVE FARM to MESSINES - ROSSIGNOL road.	
	5 pm.	1st & 3rd batteries arrived. 2nd & 3rd batteries occupied positions	S/b

Army Form C. 2118.

WAR DIARY
or
INTELLIGENCE SUMMARY.
(Erase heading not required.)

Instructions regarding War Diaries and Intelligence Summaries are contained in F.S. Regs., Part II. and the Staff Manual respectively. Title pages will be prepared in manuscript.

Hour, Date, Place		Summary of Events and Information	Remarks and references to Appendices
NEUVE EGLISE	6th April/15. 10.15 am.	1st Battery registered points in Sector B. i.e. from MESSINES - ROSSIGNOL ROAD to MESSINES - WULVERGHEM road. Their line was obtained from the map & worked out dead true.	
	12 noon	3rd Battery registered Sector A. Fuzes erratic especially in latter case. This carefully checked by an officer.	2/5.
	2.30 pm.	1st Battery registered Sector A. Observing from BURNTOUT DUG-OUT. Telephones working well.	
	9 pm.	3rd Battery reported action in action.	
7th April/15.	10 am.	3rd Battery registered Sector A.	
	11.30 am.	2nd Battery engaged a house where machine gun is reported. 2 direct hits.	
	12.15 pm.	3rd Battery shelled. Enemy employed searching fire at 50 metre intervals. 1 round fell 30'+ from battery. Direction of battery 57" true. The same of shelling was a premature from 27" 15 Battery 200x in front. No damage. Tactical command was assumed by COL BALFOUR from No. 24 Mobile at midnight 7/5. All billets are shared with 27" Mobile & there is rather a squash.	2/5.
8th April/15		A quiet day. 3rd Battery registered but fuzes poor.	2/5.
	2.30 pm.	1st Battery registered, fuzes better but range 600 + shorter. A cold windy day. Hail & rain.	

WAR DIARY
or
INTELLIGENCE SUMMARY.
(Erase heading not required.)

Army Form C. 2118.

Instructions regarding War Diaries and Intelligence Summaries are contained in F. S. Regs., Part II. and the Staff Manual respectively. Title pages will be prepared in manuscript.

Hour, Date, Place	Summary of Events and Information	Remarks and references to Appendices
NEUVE EGLISE		
9th April/15 10 a.m.	A quiet day. 2nd 15.5 fired in morning results reported good.	
3 p.m.	1st Battery started night lines. 27th Brigade left today & marched towards ST ELOI. Billets more comfortable.	2/6
11.45 p.m.	Rail Infy complained we were shelling their trenches but we were not firing. The N. mid: divs.	
10th April/15	We now have an allowance of 3 rounds per gun per day. Generally 1 battery rests & 2 fire 15 rounds a piece. Notice that 27 Inf. Bde have gone we find our own F.O.O. We gave out at dusk to Inf. H.Q. Headquarters at LA PLUS DOUVE FARM & stays till nearly light when she moves to LE ROSSIGNOL, a good arrangement in case of a night attack. He returns home at dusk.	
10 a.m.	1st Bty searched for a battery reported by aeroplane N of MESSINES. Enemy replied with H.O. 4.2 shell round of LEUWICK F.M. Little or no damage. Afternoon quiet of 1 German. Many English aeroplanes about & numbers of 1 German, the first, German planes never seen round here.	
6.15 p.m.	2nd Battery fired to find difference in corrector from the day. None obtained.	2/6
11th April/15 10.30 a.m.	3rd Battery fired Fuzes better but still unsatisfactory. A quiet afternoon. Many English aeroplanes about & numbers of 1 German, the first, German planes never seen round here. 2 German stationary balloons up but at very long range over 10,000 x	2/6

WAR DIARY
or
INTELLIGENCE SUMMARY.
(Erase heading not required.)

Army Form C. 2118.

Hour, Date, Place		Summary of Events and Information	Remarks and references to Appendices
NEUVE EGLISE			
11th April	5.20 pm	1st battery retaliated on N°4 as result of heavy rifle fire on one of our aeroplanes	9b
12th April	10 am	2nd battery retaliated on N°5. Germans fire ceased.	
	10.45 – 12.15	Germans shelled PETITE PONT & this switched & increased till 1 shell fell in N°2 horse lines. Horses had just been got clear in time. Shell fell under a saddle, threw it some feet into the air but did no damage at all. Guns appeared to be 4.2. Fuzes picked up were at 16/5	
	5 pm.	4.2.7/5 both fell on graze. Two more fell about 5pm. one was only 100x from Brigade office. This was in reply to shots from our 6" some 500 yds further on.	
	5.10 pm.	3rd Battery fired. Fuzes abominable. No "forward" observations as he had gone to ground, his farm being heavily shelled. This gun caused retaliatory fire which did some damage & we stopped. It is thought probable that the guns firing on us today are on motors.	
13th April		Busy improving cover & dug-outs. "Forward" again shelled heavily. Lt GEDYE out on telephone wires all day. System greatly improved to previous system taken over.	9b

Forms/C. 2118/10

Army Form C. 2118.

WAR DIARY
or
INTELLIGENCE SUMMARY.
(Erase heading not required.)

Hour, Date, Place	Summary of Events and Information	Remarks and references to Appendices
NEUVE EGLISE		
14th April/15	A very quiet day, no shelling either side. Suspicious details received re Estaminet 30y from 3rd b[attery] position. Report to R.a.H.Q.	
6.30 p.m.	Lamp signalling reported from house near 1st b[atter]y wagon line, shall be watched.	PØ
15th April/15	Quiet day. Gen. BUTLER inspected positions & observation stations in morning.	9/6
7.30 p.m.	Signalling observed from farm mentioned yesterday. Place surrounded & searched, men handed over to Gendarmerie.	
NIEPPE		
16th April/15 10.30 a.m.	1st battery fired on Helio in Reg; 5 Farm searched by Gendarmes but nothing found. Place watched 4 German fire.	9/6
10 p.m.	men released. No German fire.	9/6
17th April/15	Quiet morning. 2 stationary balloons up as before. O.C. 5" Warwicks reported enemy shelling thin St Farm.	
2.30 p.m.	2nd battery fired on trenches opposite B.4. Enemy's fire ceased. "Forward" shelled 3.30–4.15 & 4.45–5 pm.	9/6
18th April/15	Quiet morning.	9/6
3.30 p.m.	1st battery registered night lines & 3rd b[atter]y at 5 pm. No hostile fire.	9/6

WAR DIARY
or
INTELLIGENCE SUMMARY.
(Erase heading not required.)

Army Form C. 2118.

Hour, Date, Place		Summary of Events and Information	Remarks and references to Appendices
NEOVE EGLISE	19th April/15	Quiet day. 1st & 3rd Batteries changed map on Divn. Prepared new position for 3rd Battery	2/Lt
	20th April 4.30 p.m. 7.30 p.m.	3rd Battery digging. Germans shelled trenches 2, 3 & 4. 1st & 15g replied. 3rd & 15g left old position & were in new position by 9 p.m.	2/Lt.
	21st April/15	Very quiet day. 2nd regulated night lines. No reply. Rations so good under "Divn" became so bad under I.M. that urgent representations had to be made to H.Q. They have now improved & are excellent again and sufficient.	2/Lt.
	22nd April/15	Wonderfully quiet. 12 Officers lecture at aerodrome on co-operation of artillery & aircraft. Captive balloon up all day so unable to fire. CAPT. KELLAR (Forward) located German Battery bearing 20° True. Premature & flash light seen.	2/Lt.
	23rd April/15 10am 4 pm	Light very bad. 3rd Bty tried to register but gave up. 3rd 15g registered 1, 2 & 4. Orders had only to fire Fuze No 63 which were spired in England & that on Percussion only. Result had fuzes & about quarts of good shell	2/Lt. 2/Lt.

Army Form C. 2118.

WAR DIARY
or
INTELLIGENCE SUMMARY.
(Erase heading not required.)

Instructions regarding War Diaries and Intelligence Summaries are contained in F.S. Regs., Part II. and the Staff Manual respectively. Title pages will be prepared in manuscript.

Hour, Date, Place	Summary of Events and Information	Remarks and references to Appendices
NEUVE EGLISE. 24/4/15. 4.30–5.30 pm.	Each battery fired 30 rounds registering. Very poor results only 1 shell in 10 burst. Rest blind. MAJ. TODD (Forward) located battery in O.32.a.5.5. Germans shelled all trenches heavily.	S/6.
25th April	Germans shell trenches 8, 9 & 10 in morning & WULVERGHEM. NEUVE EGLISE & LA HUTTE ridge in afternoon. 3rd battery fired but only observed 3 rounds out of	
5 pm.	31. All rest blind. There SP 63 fuzes should never have been ordered to be fired. Their waste. The earliest 24 hours since our arrival.	S/6.
26th April.	Generally a quiet day. No hostile shell in our area. Considerable firing N and N.W. in the evening, all batteries fired in afternoon. Fuzes (as usual) hopeless. Germans seen moving road S.E. of MESSINES & telephone wires also seen running to a farm (BELHEEN)	S/6.
27th April 5 pm.	Gen BUTLER visited positions in the morning. Tried to register BELHEEN FM. None observed. English aeroplane chased German & drove him home, but not before he had dropped 2 Green lights over trenches 1&3, when Germans immediately shelled allied trenches.	S/6.

(9 29 6) W 4141—463 100,000 9/14 HWV Forms/C. 2118/10

WAR DIARY or INTELLIGENCE SUMMARY.

Army Form C. 2118.

(Erase heading not required.)

Hour, Date, Place	Summary of Events and Information	Remarks and references to Appendices
NEUVE EGLISE 28th April	A quiet morning. Enemy aeroplane flew over our lines & dropped bombs on our bivouac.	
4 pm.	2nd Battery registered BELHEEN with 11 of 65 fuzes (2 torn over) then tried another point with S/D 63, no result.	
5 pm.	10.4.2 shell put into NEUVE EGLISE, H.E. shrapnel. Only damage to material. "Forward" nearly burnt out. 3 farms in neighbourhood set on fire but not seen.	9B
29 April 11.15am	Enemy put 59 shell (4.2 probably) in Jesus Bon East (& neighbourhood) of 2nd Battery position. Farm hit 8 or 9 times.	
1 pm.	11 shell put into NEUVE EGLISE.	
4 pm.	1st Battery opened on believed Arty observing station. Observation balloon up in V.10.a.E (prob.) from 11am to 1pm. 9 2:30 - 3:45 pm	9B
30th April	Reconnaissance of S.H.R. Positions with Bde-Major (MAT. A. MURRAY-SMITH)	
3 pm.	1st & 3rd Batteries tried to register night lines. Difficulties with these fuzes.	9B

A.Barton
LT. COLONEL,
COMMANDING,
1/1st S. MIDLAND F.A. BRIGADE.

181/5610

48th Division

1st D.M. Bde R.F.A.

Volume 1 — 31.5.15

CONFIDENTIAL.

War Diary

of

1st South Midland Brigade R.F.A.

from 1/5/15 to 31/5/15

Volume X

A. Beaufort
LT. COLONEL,
COMMANDING,
1/1st S. MIDLAND F.A. BRIGADE.

WAR DIARY of 1st J.M. Bde R.F.A.

INTELLIGENCE SUMMARY.
(Erase heading not required.)

Army Form C. 2118.

Instructions regarding War Diaries and Intelligence Summaries are contained in F.S. Regs., Part II. and the Staff Manual respectively. Title pages will be prepared in manuscript.

Hour, Date, Place		Summary of Events and Information	Remarks and references to Appendices
NEUVE EGLISE	1st May 9 a.m.	2 Officers & 2 N.C.O. first party taken to see G.H.Q. positions	
	3 p.m.	all batteries registered night lines (30 rounds) all "fired" No 63 guns condemned	2/b
	2nd May	Our quietest day to date till 3.30 p.m. when intermittent shelling began. German observation station reported 0.32.c.7.5.	2/b
	3rd May	A good deal of hostile shelling	
	9 – 1 p.m.	4. Little Willies round LEUWERKFm	
	10 a.m.	18 white shrapnel on to .55	
	1.30 p.m.	6 " " " NEUVE EGLISE	
	1.30 – 2 p.m.	10 Little Willies near 3rd Bty	
	9 p.m. to 11.30 p.m.	20 " " " "	
		1st & 2nd Btys fired on obs: station	
	6 p.m.	27th Bty came into action 400 yds S. of H.Q. Office & came under fire.	2/b
	4th May	Quiet day. Rained in afternoon. 27 Bty registered PETITE DOUVE	2/b
	5th "	Quiet on the whole. 1st & 2nd registered BELLHEEN Fm.	2/b
	6th " 6.30 a.m.	0 shell fell in NEUVE EGLISE. Then 9 a.m. onwards constant shelling of our trenches. Reconnaissance of Subsidiary Positions	2/b
	7th "	Reconnaissance of O.H.Q. observation stations. Intermittent shelling of 2nd & 3rd Btys positions. No damage. Retaliated for fire on our trenches & they stopped	2/b

WAR DIARY

Army Form C. 2118.

1st S. M. Brigade R.F.A

INTELLIGENCE SUMMARY.

(Erase heading not required.)

Instructions regarding War Diaries and Intelligence Summaries are contained in F.S. Regs., Part II. and the Staff Manual respectively. Title pages will be prepared in manuscript.

Hour, Date, Place	Summary of Events and Information	Remarks and references to Appendices
NEUVE EGLISE 8th May	Quiet day. We retaliated at 2pm & enemy stopped.	2/5.
9th "	Demonstration in front of division. 11.30 – 12.30 pm fired 12 rounds per battery & 60 rounds between 6 & 7 pm. The real attack was down South near FESTUBERT apparently. Our infantry continued firing during the night.	2/5.
10th " 11 am.	Checked night lines which were too far to left. corrected	2/5.
11th "	Quiet day. Brands in NEUVE EGLISE at 11 am. BRIG.— GEN. ROSS-JOHNSON visited brigade observing station on assuming command.	2/5.
12th "	Quite quiet. No shelling	2/5.
13th "	Quiet. 8 rounds in NEUVE EGLISE	2/5.
14th "	Quiet. 10 rounds in " "	2/5.
15th " 11 am. 3.15 pm & 5 pm.	Germans shelled our trenches. We replied each time & they stopped. 9 rounds (6 blind) into village. (N.E.) Commenced preparation of J.H.Q. positions. 2 Canadian officers arrived to reconnoitre 2 positions to relieve 27th Bde	2/5.
16th 12 noon	Retaliated with 12 rounds opposite trench No 70. Bromans into village. 2 Canadians left & MAJ. POSTON & BROUSSON arrived to occupy 2 positions vice canadians.	2/5.

(9 29 6) W 4141—463 100,000 9/14 H W V Forms/C. 2118/10

Army Form C. 2118.

WAR DIARY

INTELLIGENCE SUMMARY.

(Erase heading not required.)

Instructions regarding War Diaries and Intelligence Summaries are contained in F.S. Regs., Part II. and the Staff Manual respectively. Title pages will be prepared in manuscript.

Hour, Date, Place	Summary of Events and Information	Remarks and references to Appendices
NEUVE EGLISE 17th May	Wet morning. Abominable light. No shooting. Reconnoitred positions with B2 Bty of K's army. C + D 51st Bde.	2/5
18th May 11 pm	Wet + misty day. Bad light. 27th Bde. Byt. C/51 + D/51 due 9 pm. but did not arrive till 11.15 pm. Result clashed with 27th Bde. CAPT STONE + LT ESTCOURT sent to help find them. Reported in action C/51 at 1.30 am. D/51 at 3.30 am. LIEUT WELLS and NOYES 23rd DIV. attached for 14 days course.	2/5
19th "	Very bad light. Quiet.	2/5
20th "	Again bad light + quiet. 1st + 3rd batteries withdrawn + A/51 + B/51 occupy their positions. COL. CARTER andy 51st Bde takes over tactical command.	2/5
21st "	2nd Bty engaged working party. Ammunition real bad, many rounds failed to burst tho' gun's fuze could be heard. Target gunners in shell.	2/5
22nd	Nothing of note	2/5
23rd	ditto	2/5
24th	ditto	1/5

Army Form C. 2118.

WAR DIARY
1st / 1 m Kole RFA

or
INTELLIGENCE SUMMARY.
(Erase heading not required.)

Instructions regarding War Diaries and Intelligence Summaries are contained in F.S. Regs., Part II. and the Staff Manual respectively. Title pages will be prepared in manuscript.

Hour, Date, Place	Summary of Events and Information	Remarks and references to Appendices
NEUVE EGLISE. 25th May	Nothing to report. Subsidiary a S.A.A. munitions finished	9/6
26th "	Nothing to report. Light very good again.	4/6
27th "	Selected & occupied new observing station on SS for 2nd By and HQ	I/6.
28th "	3rd Bty in future will return to Trench sh/91 to observe. The Hrees coming out have made observation very difficult. sh/91 Bty now observes from SS also	I/6.
29th "	Quiet. 6 5.9 How. into NEUVE EGLISE. First time shell over 4.2 been fired into the village.	I/6.
30th "	20 rounds into & round village. One fell 120⁺ from this billet.	I/6.
31st "	3rd Bty observing station selected on SS. Shell we have are very old mostly made 1900 –1901. dated 1901 + 02. Cartridges 1899–1901. Fuzes are 9/.906. Occasionally we find shell	✗

E.B. Amberton
LT. COLONEL.
COMMANDING.
1/1st S. MIDLAND F.A. BRIGADE.

a 2
ag 2

109/59w

48th Division.

1st S.M. Bde R.F.A.

Vol IV 1 — 30.6.15

CONFIDENTIAL.

WAR DIARY
of
1st South Midland Brigade R.F.A.

From 1st June 1915 To 30th June 1915.

Volume XI

A.W. Balfour
Lieut-Colonel R.F.A.
Commanding 1st S.M. Brigade R.F.A.

WAR DIARY of 1st South Midland / Sale R.G.A.

INTELLIGENCE SUMMARY.

(Erase heading not required.)

Army Form C. 2118.

Hour, Date, Place	Summary of Events and Information	Remarks and references to Appendices
NEUVE EGLISE 1st June/15	A quiet day. Nothing to report.	I/S
2nd June	Nothing to report.	I/S
3rd June	Quite quiet. C.O. & adjt. went round subsidiary line with reconnd. by Kate Smith & his Bde. Major.	I/S
4th June 10 pm	5th Brigade withdrew & 1st & 3rd Batteries returned to their old positions. B/50 took over position near this office & came under tactical orders of O.C. Brigade.	2/S
11 pm	All batteries in position & lines laid.	
5th June	The Germans have recently brought up some new guns on this front. At least 2 5.9 Howitzers & 2 French 3".7 guns have been recognized but not located. In the afternoon they put 7 or 2 round 3rd Bty. One hit a dugout & splinters hit a man but otherwise no damage. They then set fire to farm in front of the battery (not it) & sent them 70-100 shells.	2/S
3.45 pm		
6th June	Nothing of interest except some 30 rounds were just normal the observing stations on 55. opinions differ as to whether 4".2 or bigger. Our working party were relieved.	2/S
7th June	A good deal of spasmodic shelling of our trenches to which we replied, twice with effect on to the batteries located by aeroplane in O.33.a. In the afternoon a working party was located in O.32.c. & successfully engaged.	2/S

Army Form C. 2118.

WAR DIARY
or
INTELLIGENCE SUMMARY.
(Erase heading not required.)

Hour, Date, Place	Summary of Events and Information	Remarks and references to Appendices
NEUVE EGLISE 8th June 6.45 p.m.	A working party observed N. of BELLHEEM FARM U.3.B.0.2 & engaged. This party was observed in the evening & was	
7.15 p.m.	shelled. They appear to be creating a small hut for screen. A quiet day on the whole.	3/5
10 p.m.	B/63 relieved B/50. 2nd Lt WALLACE in command.	
9th June 8 a.m.	B/63 registered PETITE DOUVE. In the afternoon intermittent shelling of WULVERGHEM ROAD, PLUG STREET WOOD, NEUVE EGLISE & round "55". Otherwise very quiet. We have not fired. Light very bad.	3/5
10th June 11 a.m.	Had thunderstorm during the night. German mine exploded outside Plug Street but did not disturb us. Light very bad till 5.30 p.m. Then Germans started shelling all along our line & on WULVERGHEM ROAD. We retaliated as	
5.45 p.m.	long as we could. They fired some 60 4.2 all told up to dark.	3/5
11th June 8-11.30	Intermittent shelling of WULVERGHEM Road & neighbourhood	
3 p.m.	6 rds in NEUVE EGLISE. Intern more or less steady shelling all afternoon. Some 130 rounds in this area.	3/5
12th June 1.45 a.m.	3rd Battery false alarm 7½ minutes from standing in manage to 1st Gun. Must improve. Fairly quiet Reconnaissance by CO + Adjt of forward wire cutting positions.	3/5

(9 20 6) W 4141—463 100,000 9/14 HWV Forms/C.2118/10

Army Form C. 2118.

WAR DIARY of 1st 7.m. Bde 1854
INTELLIGENCE SUMMARY.
(Erase heading not required.)

Hour, Date, Place		Summary of Events and Information	Remarks and references to Appendices
NEUVE EGLISE	13th June 3 am	3rd RB false alarm. Soon reduced to 4½ minutes	
	14th	Not good enough. A quiet day. Village shelled time 10 secs.	2/6
		A quiet day on the whole. In conjunction with mortars	
	6.45 pm	shelled farm 0.32.c.6.1. Village (Neuve Eglise) shelled in afternoon	
		shells pitching further up. Time 11 secs. Battery no in 0.33.a.me think.	2/6
	15th	A quiet day. Afternoon reconnaissance of wire cutting positions	2/6 2/5
	16th	Quiet. Tested new fuze (No 80) corrector found to be same	2/6 2/5
		as for No 65	2/6 2/5
	17th	Quiet. Nothing to record	2/6 2/5
	18th	Very quiet indeed. Further reconnaissance of wire cutting positions	2/6 2/5
	19th	Quite quiet.	2/5
	20th	Working Party located in U.2.a.5.W. shelled. Otherwise quiet	2/5
	21st	Battery shelled NEUVE EGLISS & located in 0.32.d.	2/6 2/5
	22nd	Very quiet	2/6 2/5
	23rd	Nothing to report	2/6 2/5
	23/24/24th	As usual quiet quiet. 2 Canadian officers arrived to take over	2/5
	25th	2 Heavy thunderstorms. Quiet.	2/5
	26th	Quiet. Handed over during the day to 2nd Canadian Brigade	
OUTERSTEENE	10 pm 27th	R.F.A. & then marched via BAILLEUL to OUTTERSTEENE arriving at 2 am. All reports show our front from PETIT DOUVE FARM to WULVERGHEM – MESSINES ROAD has at all times been held by BAVARIANS. HWV	

Army Form C. 2118.

WAR DIARY

of 1st South Midland Bde R.F.A.

INTELLIGENCE SUMMARY.

(Erase heading not required.)

Hour, Date, Place	Summary of Events and Information	Remarks and references to Appendices
OUTTERSTEENE. 27th June 9 p.m.	A good billet. In evening Bde. marched to VIEUX BERQUIN arriving about 11 p.m. & there billeted. The Brigade is now part of Group "C" under B.G.C. 144th Inf. Bde. with which it is now marching. Groups "A" & "B" marched 2 & 1 day ahead respectively. Each Group is self-contained with a company R.E. & A.S.C. & a section of Field Ambulance. Rain during afternoon but fine march.	J/16.
VIEUX BERQUIN 28th 6 p.m. 11.15 p.m.	Good billets at 6 p.m. Bde. marched via MERVILLE to ROBECQ arriving about 11.15 p.m. & billeted for the night. A good march with occasional rain. Nothing bad.	J/16.
ROBECQ 29th 6 p.m.	Rained on and off during the day. Not bad. Good billets. Marched via LILLERS to FERFAY arriving about 11.15 p.m. Billeted in Chateau, battery lines in Chateau Grounds. 2 heavy storms during march. Good billet but water 1½ miles away rather spoils it. B.G.C. & inspected Bde. on line of march.	J/16.
FERFAY. 30th	Occasional rain in morning. Day spent in inspections etc. No casualties of any sort during the march to men or horses. Very satisfactory	J/16.

A. Balfour
Lieut-Colonel R.F.A.
Comdg 1st S.M. Brigade R.F.A.

121/6341

48th Division

1st S.M. Bde R.T.A.
Part I
1-31-7-15

CONFIDENTIAL.

War Diary

of

1st South Midland Brigade R.F.A.

from 1st July 1915 to 31st July 1915.

(VOLUME XII.)

AubBeaufor
Lt. Colonel,
Comdg.
1st S. Midland FA Bde.

WAR DIARY of 1st South Midland Bde R.F.A.

INTELLIGENCE SUMMARY

Army Form C. 2118.

(Erase heading not required.)

Hour, Date, Place	Summary of Events and Information	Remarks and references to Appendices
FERFAY. 1st July/15.	The day was spent in inspections & general cleaning up.	J/5
2nd	1st & 2nd Batteries inspection in marching order.	J/5
3rd	3rd Battery & Ammunition Column inspection in marching order	J/5
4th Sunday	Quiet day for all ranks. Church Parade in morning.	J/5
5th	LIEUT A.C.R. CROOME-JOHNSON returned from course at Trench Mortar School. Reconnaissance of positions for night "Exercise" with 145th Inf: Brigade in woods E of ALLOUAGNE.	J/5
Omitted from 27th June/15	LIEUT A.C.R. CROOME-JOHNSON left for course at Trench Mortar School ST. VENANT.	J/5
6th	Reconnaissance of routes to starting points in case of attack. Use of fields for drill.	J/5
6 p.m.	Officers & Telephonists left to take part in Exercise with Infantry. LIEUT A.C.R. CROOME-JOHNSON left to take command of Trench Mortar Battery. Leave for 1 Officer & 3 men per Bde sanctioned.	J/5
7th 4.30 a.m.	Night operations over & all returned to billets. Usual drills. All units route march.	J/5
8th		J/5
9th	Usual drills. Reconnaissance of 1st Div positions by C.O. & Adjt	J/5
10th	Usual drills. MAJ. BROWNE on reconnaissance with Infantry.	J/5
11th Sunday	Church Parade & Camp inspections. Reconnaissance of advanced 2nd Line Positions. 2nd LIEUT B.G. JAMES left for attachment (on probation) to R.F.C.	J/5

WAR DIARY
of 1st S.M. Bde. R.F.A.
INTELLIGENCE SUMMARY.
(Erase heading not required.)

Army Form C. 2118.

Hour, Date, Place		Summary of Events and Information	Remarks and references to Appendices
FERFAY	12th July/15. 1 pm.	3.N.C.O's, Restaurance officers & N.C.O orderly officer proceeded to MAZINGARBE to take over positions from 47th Divn.	
	2 pm.	1 section from each battery left for same place. They marched via HOUCHIN & reached MAZINGARBE at 11.15. The column	
	6 pm.	then halted till 12.30 am. When the column returned to FERFAY	
13th July	12.30 am.	arriving back at 10.30 am.	J.B.
	9 am.	The platoon, which had remained behind, had Driving Drill on the Common (a big field belonging to French Govt)	
	10.30 am.	2 LIEUT W.A. TODD transferred from Amm Column to 2nd Battery. This Brigade now belongs to 4th Corps, 1st Army together with 1st Division & 47th (2nd London) Division.	J.B.
14th July	10 am.	One battery driving drill & reconputation of positions.	J.B.
15th July	10 am.	ditto — Notified that Bde is to be at once re-equipped with 15 pr Q.F. Great rejoicings.	J.B.
16th July	10 am.	One battery as above.	2.B.
17th July		Usual drills. CAPT BOYCE left for billeting in new area.	J.B.
18th "		Preparing to move	J.B.
19th "	5 am.	2 LIEUT LANE & 4 NCOs left for billeting area.	
	6 pm.	Bde H.Q. & 1st Battery left CHATEAU D'HNNISDAL, FERFAY Left LILLERS station.	J.B.

WAR DIARY

INTELLIGENCE SUMMARY.

of 1st A.M. Bde RFA

Army Form C. 2118.

(Erase heading not required.)

Instructions regarding War Diaries and Intelligence Summaries are contained in F.S. Regs., Part II. and the Staff Manual respectively. Title pages will be prepared in manuscript.

Hour, Date, Place		Summary of Events and Information	Remarks and references to Appendices
LILLERS	20th July 3 a.m.	2nd Battery left station by train for MONDICOURT	
	7 a.m.	3rd Battery — do —	
	5.40 p.m.	Amm Column — do —	
MONDICOURT	20th July 6.30 a.m.	The Brigade arrived & detrained at the following hours:— Bde. H.Q. & 1st Battery	
	11.30 a.m.	2nd Battery	
	3.15 p.m.	3rd Battery	
	21st July 11 a.m.	Ammunition Column	
THIÈVRES		After detraining the Brigade marched to billets at THIÈVRES (M. LEFEBVRE)	
	6 a.m.	Brigade drew 12.15 pr. Q.F. Guns & 3.6 Amm. Wagons (8 per Battery) + 12 for A.C.) from DOULLENS. 7th Corps Commander (LIEUT.GEN. SNOW) 4 R.G.A. inspected the lines CAPT BOYCE rejoined	£/5
	2 p.m.		
	4 p.m.		
22nd July		Gun Drill & Laying. Three Sergt. Instructors were lent by R. 14th J.A. Brigade for 4 days on the new gun. The division now forms part of New 7th Corps with HQ at +15th Division. The new 3rd Army (GEN MONROE) consists of 7th + 10th Corps.	£/5
23rd July		Gun Drill, Laying. Exercise	
		— ditto —	£/5
		— do —	£/5
24th "			£/5
25th "		5 Guns & 26 Wagons + 2 G.S. Wagons of 15th T.M.B.L.E. Equipment entrained at DOULLENS & Guns sent to BEAUVAL for 51st Div. Arty, & 5.J. Wagons to 4th Div A.C. & 6 to £/5 1st S.T. Div A.C.	

Army Form C. 2118.

WAR DIARY of 1st M. Bde RFA
INTELLIGENCE SUMMARY.
(Erase heading not required.)

Instructions regarding War Diaries and Intelligence Summaries are contained in F.S. Regs., Part II. and the Staff Manual respectively. Title pages will be prepared in manuscript.

Hour, Date, Place		Summary of Events and Information	Remarks and references to Appendices
THIEVRES.	26th July 6 pm.	Drills as usual. 3rd Battery left + went into action near SAILLY.	2/5
	27th "	Gun Drill. Laying etc. 2/LIEUT R.J. TAYNTON +19 men of 1st reinforcements arrived from HAVRE	2/5
	28th "	do	2/5
	29th "	Drills as usual.	2/5
	30th "	do — LIEUT-COL WISE, MAJ TODD, CAPT BOYCE	
	12 noon	9 LIEUT GEDYE left for SAILLY to prepare for arrival of the Brigade.	2/5
SAILLY	31st " 6.30 pm	The Brigade less 3rd Battery left THIEVRES for SAILLY and neighbourhood. Brigade HdQrs are at COLINCAMPS. all Battery positions about 1/2 way between COLINCAMPS and HEBUTERNE. Wagon lines & Amm Cophumn at COIGNEAUX. We are now Brigaded with 144th Inf. Bde. Batteries reported in position by 11 p.m. Splendid positions, very well dug in by French 51st Regt from whom we took over. 1st from 4th & 2nd from 3rd. 3 occupy empty positions.	2/5

48th Division

121/6561

CONFIDENTIAL

WAR DIARY
OF
1ST SOUTH MIDLAND BRIGADE, R.F.A.

from 1st August to 31st August 1915.

Volume ~~XII~~ VI

AuBaulon
LT. COLONEL,
COMMANDING,
1/1st S. MIDLAND F.A. BRIGADE.

Army Form C. 2118.

WAR DIARY
of 1st / 1 M. Hole R.T.2.
INTELLIGENCE SUMMARY.
(Erase heading not required.)

Instructions regarding War Diaries and Intelligence Summaries are contained in F.S. Regs., Part II. and the Staff Manual respectively. Title pages will be prepared in manuscript.

Hour, Date, Place	Summary of Events and Information	Remarks and references to Appendices
COLINCAMPS 1st Aug 1915.	In addition to our three batteries, the following are also under Tactical Command of 2nd Brigade :— 1st & 2nd Battery 3rd M. Brigade & 3rd Battery 2nd Hole. The whole are grouped with 14th By. Hole. Batteries registering.	J/S
2nd "	Much time occupied in laying telephone lines. Attached diagram shews communications as at present arranged. Very bad thunderstorm, swamping Bty positions, at 4 p.m. Registering.	J/S.
3rd "	Registering. The office work caused by 6 batteries colossal & quite interferes with anything else being done.	J/S.
4th "	A working party on a sap-head was successfully engaged by 2nd in the early hours. In the afternoon 3rd Bty took on Machine Gun with H.E. most successfully.	J/S.
5th "	It is such a treat having 16 guns. They are shooting splendidly & fuzes are quite good. We now know we can hit what we try to. The Infantry have remarked on the good shooting, & have twice asked for retaliation each occasion expressing satisfaction.	J/S

WAR DIARY
or
INTELLIGENCE SUMMARY.
(Erase heading not required.)

Army Form C. 2118.

of 1st S.M. Bde R.F.A.

Hour, Date, Place	Summary of Events and Information	Remarks and references to Appendices
COLIN CAMPS 6th Aug 19/15	The positions of Batteries in action are shewn on attached rough plan. Road 200 x. of 2nd Bty shelled very heavily with 6"	S/S
9.30 pm	2nd Warwick Battery withdrawn. Jones re-adjusted.	
7th Aug	1st Warwick Battery withdrawn. Further re-adjustment of Zones. Road again heavily shelled	S/S
8th "	1/2 3rd Worcester Battery withdrawn & replaced by 1/2 of 2nd Battery. This change of position by 2nd Battery was done in order to (1) be able to fire more to the right (South) (2) to bring more enfilade fire	S/S
9th "	One of the worst thunderstorms I have known. All dug-outs were badly swamped, 2 ft. of water and over in some of them. Two guns of 1st Bty had their breechs under water & were out of action for 2 hours. Remainder of Worcester Battery withdrawn & 2nd Bty completed the change of position.	S/S
10th	A quiet day ! after the storm ! The Germans generally put some 6" into this village each day but so far without damage. An 11" one round fell 10' from Bde office 4 killed	S/S
11th	A quiet day. 2 German planes over in the evening.	S/S

Army Form C. 2118.

WAR DIARY
of 1st S.M. Bde RFA
INTELLIGENCE SUMMARY.
(Erase heading not required.)

Instructions regarding War Diaries and Intelligence Summaries are contained in F.S. Regs., Part II. and the Staff Manual respectively. Title pages will be prepared in manuscript.

Hour, Date, Place	Summary of Events and Information	Remarks and references to Appendices
COLINCAMPS 12th Aug. 1915	A Quiet day. Registering continued. Trench mortar located 57I.	S/5.
13th Aug.	Nothing particular to report. The Germans are working hard on some 6 saps in our zone & we fire whenever observed, provided damage is not up.	S/5.
14th Aug. 4.30am	Engaged a sap with 2nd Bty in conjunction with 1st Howitzer Battery. Reconnoitring for observing stations to see the Right of our zone.	
11 pm.	2nd Worcester Battery in action & came under orders of O.C. Brigade. Leah allotted "A Swinger" with night lines on extreme right.	S/5.
15th Aug	Registration continued by all batteries. Reconnaissance.	S/5.
16th Aug	Nothing to report. Very little shelling in our zone.	S/5.
17th Aug	3rd Bty position shelled by 'A – B'. No damage. Central Observing Station shelled with little willies. No damage done.	S/5.
18th Aug	Very quiet. Very heavy storm in morning & light loss all day. Reconnaissance of wire cutting positions.	S/5.
19th "	Had light till 1 pm when registration was proceeded with. Ammunition limited to 158 rounds per Bde for the week. Reconnaissance continued.	S/5.

WAR DIARY of 1st South Midland Brigade R.F.A.

INTELLIGENCE SUMMARY.
(Erase heading not required.)

Army Form C. 2118.

Instructions regarding War Diaries and Intelligence Summaries are contained in F.S. Regs., Part II. and the Staff Manual respectively. Title pages will be prepared in manuscript.

Hour, Date, Place	Summary of Events and Information	Remarks and references to Appendices
COLINCAMPS. 20th Aug/15	The Germans shelled Central observing station with field guns in the morning. Flashes were observed at bearing of 93° but Maj. Todd who saw them is of opinion that they were "puffs". A field gun battery has come into action E of SERRE WOOD & probably the puffs are a blind for this new position. The barrage has changed its position further South bearing 104½. Both above bearings from Central. c.34.c.2.9.	E.B.
21st Aug/15.	All B type S.A.A. handed in. A quiet day & dull weather. No sausages up. Result very little German firing but we were able to continue our registering.	E.B.
22nd Aug/15	A considerable amount of hostile fire today. 40-50 into this village, then on to Central, then round 3rd/S.Mg then back to this village. No damage. Also 6 near COURCELLES. 3rd Mg dispersed 2 working parties just South of '57.2'. Balloon up most of day.	E.B.
23rd Aug/15	Balloon up all day. Germans fired frequently 2 or 3 rounds on to Infantry who were visible going to & fro for the late relief. Line of barrage directed by the barrage. We have no barrage of today. It was French & only once have we had any information from it. Reconnaissance of new positions by infantry	
11 p.m.	called on 3rd Mg to fire on Working Party at Bt 301. Complied with on round. Work ceased during the night.	E.B.
24th Aug/15	3rd Battery have a gun out today. It is a "pièce de serve" in action in a crop of clover. It is stabled whether the barrage is up or not. 30 rounds are dumped. We must share most on an allowance of 2 per bty per week.	

10:15 p.m.

Forms/C.2118/10
(9 29 6) W 4141—463 100,000 9/14 HWV

WAR DIARY
INTELLIGENCE SUMMARY

Army Form C. 2118.

1st S.M. Feb R.H.

Hour, Date, Place	Summary of Events and Information	Remarks and references to Appendices
COLINCAMPS 24th Aug. 1915.	The morning was very quiet, in fact the whole day, so the gun did not fire except just to check line as soon as it was light. LIEUT A.G. ALEXANDER to 1st Bty, LTS PULFORD and GUILD to 2nd and LT WEBSTER to 3rd Bty are attached for 14 days course. C.O.'s was called which thanks to people on road behind 2nd Worcester battery withdrew to its wagon line & left them command.	
9 pm.	2nd Bty fired on working Party in sqr. F.6.a.3.7. and later dispersed	
5.30 pm.	Working Party in sqr. F.6.a.5.8. Result V.S.	
11.45 pm.	Sun in sqr. 3/0.	
7.45 pm.	1st Bty fired on machine Sun in sqr. 3/0.	
6.30 pm.	" " Transport on SERRE - PUISIEUX ROAD & again at	
11 pm.	" " all above on Report of Infantry. Transport galloped off. Central was again shelled. People will walk about on the road behind. Barely a division order will stop it & fair. Cyclists use the SERRE - PUISIEUX ROAD daily 6.30 to 6.30 pm.	28
25th Aug/15	Very hazy day and observation very difficult. Reconnaissance new observing stations. It is noted how much more often the Infantry call on us for "support" now that we have Bn. Very quiet day. No movements to report. Only 4 rounds fired. The light has been very bad the last few days and no sausage has been up. Nothing could be seen till 9 am today. Another very quiet day. Line Sgt B'de took over 1st & 2nd Bty	28
26th Aug/15.		
7 am	Jones at 6 am today but we still remain covering the same top for the present. 2nd battery had a gun out but the was 2nd firing. 143rd B'de now withdrawn (1pm) and 3rd Bty cover 5th B'n O'Pos. (145th B'de)	E/b

WAR DIARY
INTELLIGENCE SUMMARY

of 1st L.M. Bde R.G.A.

(Erase heading not required.)

Army Form C. 2118.

Hour, Date, Place	Summary of Events and Information	Remarks and references to Appendices
COLIN CAMPS 26th Aug (cont) 11.35 pm	Infantry called on 2nd Battery to fire on working party on Sap 311, which was successfully complied with in 2 rounds.	J/S.
27th Aug/15 1 pm.	A quiet morning and no shooting in our zone by either side. Orders received for 1st Bty to change position at night & the Brigade to quit its old zone 314 – 301 and take up new line 304 to 150°N of B63. The Batteries will cover the zone in the following order from Right to Left. 2nd Bty, 3rd Bty, 1st Bty. The two former not having to change position registered their new night lines during the afternoon. The	
10.5 pm.	2nd Battery reported in new position (which is alongside 3rd Bty) & lines laid. All Batteries were duly in communication with their new infantry by 9 pm. During the afternoon 2nd & 3rd Sept called by Infantry to retaliate which was done most successfully.	
11 pm.	1st Battery called on to engage working Party Pt 869 but as they had not begun registering, 3rd Bty were turned on successfully.	J/S
28th Aug	1st Battery began registration of its new zone. The 1st Battery new observing station is by the Cemetery in HEBUTERNE as the direction is almost at right angles to his line of fire which takes the trenches almost in enfilade. It is excellent for observing for range but difficult for line and was found necessary to have an observer at Central to assist in the latter. A quiet day. Heavy rains at night	J/S.

Army Form C. 2118.

WAR DIARY
of 1/1st N. Mid. R.F.A.
INTELLIGENCE SUMMARY.
(Erase heading not required.)

Hour, Date, Place	Summary of Events and Information	Remarks and references to Appendices
COLINCAMPS. 29th Aug/15. afternoon.	Some 27 Little Willies fell on road between HEBUTERNE and Central during the morning. No damage. Otherwise very quiet. Some 14 more L.W's in same place as this morning. 3rd Battery registered new machine gun positions at C.30.C.9.7 and near .873. Heavy rain from 5.30 p.m. till 10 p.m. & also sharp storms during night.	EB.
30th Aug/15 @ 5am	Balloon (German) n/w L. of SERRE for 5 minutes, over our work at 3 of .B63 located. Then working driven off by 1st Battery.	
9.40am	Balloon up. 16 L.W's during morning on to CARRIERE same place as yesterday. In the afternoon they fired 5 more. Two casemates for guns located at D.32.a.6.6 and one at D.26.c.5.6	
8 p.m.	3rd Bty. called on to engage Refujo in communication trench .374	EB.
29th Aug	OMITTED FROM 29th Aug/15. ---- 2nd Lieuts. F. ELLERTON and W.F. RIDLER joined for duty from England and are attached to Ammunition Column	EB.
31st Aug/15. 11.30 p.m.	Balloon up today. Germans shelled our trenches opposite MB5 who retaliated successfully. German guns appeared to be 4.2" Germans also shelled CARRIERE again with Little Willies. Infantry	EB.
2.30 p.m.	called on 1st Bty. and also fired very brisk in our sector during the afternoon + evening. Bursts of Red lights at 8.1 pm & 11.36 p.m. but nothing noted afterwards.	EB.

AW Balfour
LT. COLONEL,
COMMANDING,
1/1st S. MIDLAND F.A. BRIGADE.

1st Sept. 1915

48th Division

CONFIDENTIAL

121/6973

WAR DIARY

OF

1st SOUTH MIDLAND BRIGADE R.F.A.

From September 1st to September 30th. 1915.

VOLUME ~~XIV~~ VII

[signature]
LT. COLONEL,
COMMANDING,
1/1st S. MIDLAND F.A. BRIGADE.

XIV (i)

Army Form C. 2118.

WAR DIARY
of 1st South Midland Brigade Regt.

INTELLIGENCE SUMMARY.
(Erase heading not required.)

Instructions regarding War Diaries and Intelligence Summaries are contained in F.S. Regs., Part II. and the Staff Manual respectively. Title pages will be prepared in manuscript.

Hour, Date, Place	Summary of Events and Information	Remarks and references to Appendices
COLINCAMPS 1st Sept 1915 11 am.	A quiet morning. 2nd Bty has a "pièce de servir" out. 7 men Reinforcements arrived. All Drivers, 1 for 3rd Bty, 6 for A.C. Balloon up at 7.15am down 12.30pm when it clouded over. Very wet from 2pm onwards. It seems almost certain that an 6" Howitzer has just come up against us. Quiet evening.	JB
2nd Sept	1st Bty has a gun out. A few 5.9"0 in this direction about 11 am but did not reach the village. Cloudy morning & frequent showers of rain. Only very little field gun firing in our zone in afternoon. Smoke from 2 trains seen in ACHIET-	
3.30 pm	LE-PETIT. German transport ↔ & working parties loading	
4.15/pm	up wagons seen W. of same village.	JB
COLINCAMPS 3rd Sept 1 pm.	Very quiet morning. No firing in our zone. Bde HQ. closed here & opened at new billet at HEBUTERNE. All wires to Bertrat cut by ↔ Little rallies during the afternoon	JB
HEBUTERNE 4th Sept	Intermittent shelling of our trenches and CARRIÈRE.	
2.25 pm	2nd engaged working Party T 6 B 7.5 successfully & later 3rd retaliated for so little railing.	JB
	Smoke observed coming from casemates D 32. a. 5. 6.	
5th Sept 8 30 am.	3rd retaliated by ragout of infantry with 6 rounds. Hostile fire appeared to come from .909 N.E. of SERRE. Work seen in progress in trench 3.1.a.F.E during afternoon & also men working on fields near 311. Reconnaissance of wire setting position	JB

XIV (ii)

Army Form C. 2118.

WAR DIARY of 1/5 J. M. Bde 1914
or
INTELLIGENCE SUMMARY.

(Erase heading not required.)

Instructions regarding War Diaries and Intelligence Summaries are contained in F.S. Regs., Part II. and the Staff Manual respectively. Title pages will be prepared in manuscript.

Hour, Date, Place	Summary of Events and Information	Remarks and references to Appendices
HEBUTERNE 6th Sept	Hostile fire in our front from 12 noon 5th to 12 noon 6th for 1st time. A good deal of work has been done on E side of PUISIEUX-SERRE road the past few days. Two horsemen & 2 working parties seen in J.3.	S/6.
7th Sept 5 am	The four officers attached to Battery left for England again.	
7 am	Working party stopped by 1st R&B in C.30 & 9.1. In afternoon 3rd Bty established opposite Trench 29.	S/6.
8th Sept 9.30 am	German flare over Central 9.30 am & 11.48 am. 2nd Bty stopped working party in C.29 d.10.3	
1 pm	3rd engaged machine gun successfully with N.2. Leg regiment of infantry	
12.45 pm	1st retaliated on request of infantry.	S/6.
2.30 & 5.20 pm		
9th Sept	Quiet until 10 am. A quiet day. Lieuts ELLERTON & RIDLER attached to 3rd & 1st Btys respectively.	S/6.
10th Sept	Hostile aeroplanes very active in morning, 3 over at once. A quiet day. Amm Column moved to AUTHIE and are billeted there.	S/6.
11th Sept	A quiet day. HEBUTERNE shelled 8-9.30 pm. 3rd retaliated. No casualties by ourselves. All batteries now have billets in this village.	S/6.
12th Sept 2.45 pm	3rd Bty retaliated on Trenches opposite Trench 25 by request of infantry. Intermittent shelling in afternoon into HEBUTERNE and round Battery positions. 2nd successfully engaged working party in Sylvian area by request of Irish infantry.	S/6.
13th Sept	A quiet day. Completion of reconnaissance of wire-cutting positions.	S/6.

XIV. (iii)

Army Form C. 2118.

Instructions regarding War Diaries and Intelligence Summaries are contained in F.S. Regs., Part II. and the Staff Manual respectively. Title pages will be prepared in manuscript.

WAR DIARY
of 1st J.M. Brigade R.F.A.

INTELLIGENCE SUMMARY.
(Erase heading not required.)

Hour, Date, Place	Summary of Events and Information	Remarks and references to Appendices
HEBUTERNE 14th Sept	Quiet morning. Occasional shells on S. edge of Hebuterne. Nothing	
9 pm.	to report for afternoon. 175th preparing wire cutting position. A gun is out every day now. 175th Mondays & Thursdays. 2nd Tuesdays & Fridays. 3rd Wednesdays & Saturdays.	E/b
15th Sept	Quiet morning. MAJ LATTEY of 2nd J.M. Bde, preparing wire cutting position for 1 section of his battery to be attached to us. Germans shelled this village 12.55 to 1.15 p.m. we retaliated successfully on PUISIEUX & they stopped. They put 6 more in at 5.30 p.m. but did no damage.	E/b
16th Sept	Conference of O.C.s & adjts by C.R.A. Quiet morning and afternoon.	E/b
17th Sept 9.45 am	O.C. 1st located battery by smoke in D.26.a. N.E. it had been putting a few shell just N. of this village.	E/b
3.15 pm.	3.15-30 p.m. put into this village. We retaliated on PUISIEUX & the Howitzers on GOMIECOURT WOOD. Germans stopped firing into 1st & 3rd Btys. No damage.	
18th Sept. 9 am.	Fired a few gun flatteries on to 1st & 3rd Btys signals	
5.30 pm	3 rounds into this village. We put 9 into PUISIEUX	E/b
	4 " " " " " " " " 6 " "	
19th Sept	Otherwise quiet day	E/b
	The Germans did a good deal more shelling than usual but nevertheless it was very indiscriminate. Quiet afternoon.	E/b

XIV. (iv).

Army Form C. 2118.

WAR DIARY
of 1st S. M. Bde R.F.A.
INTELLIGENCE SUMMARY.
(Erase heading not required.)

Instructions regarding War Diaries and Intelligence Summaries are contained in F.S. Regs., Part II. and the Staff Manual respectively. Title pages will be prepared in manuscript.

Place	Hour, Date	Summary of Events and Information	Remarks and references to Appendices
HEBUTERNE	20th Sept	A quiet day in our zone. Lost replenishment of ammunition by C.R.A.	E/B
	21st Sept 5.30pm	Conference of C.O's + Adjutants by C.R.A. at H.Q. 2nd Bde	
	11 am		
	3pm. 3.30pm	Shelled PUISIEUX 60 rounds in all. Germans retaliated on this village at 6 pm. with 40 rounds (about) but not	
	5.45pm 6 pm.	after the evening shoot. 2nd Lieut. J.D.CHALLE attached from 158th Bde R.F.A.	E/B
	22nd Sept	A quiet morning in our zone. Also afternoon.	
	23rd " 11 am	Conference of B.C's + Adjutants by C.R.A. at H.Q. 2nd Bde.	
	3 pm	1st Bty shelled B69 with 37 rounds & LA LOUVIERE Fme with 60 H.E., 2nd Battery communication trench B77, with 40 shrapnel. 3rd Bty B63 with 20 shrapnel in conjunction with 4th S.M. (How) Bde.	
	4/pm	1st Bty wire cutting B73 & 2nd Bty at 301 each 75 rds shrapnel. The latter was V.S.; results of former difficult to see owing to poor light. 3rd Bty 40 H.E. on B63 & rounds & Shrapnel from 2nd Bty into PUISIEUX, 3rd Bty 20 shrapnel	
	5 pm	(B71) in conjunction with howitzers. 1st Bty finished ammunition allotted at 3 pm on same fronts. The Germans fired very little retaliation. None into this village. 3rd Bty had one casualty, wounded. 2nd Bty moved to 1st Bty position & 1st Bty moved to wire cutting position at C.28.d.2.4. New maps received & to come into action with new lettering on 27th.	E/B

XIV. (V.)

Army Form C. 2118.

WAR DIARY
of J/1st J.M. Bde R.F.A.
INTELLIGENCE SUMMARY.
(Erase heading not required.)

Instructions regarding War Diaries and Intelligence Summaries are contained in F.S. Regs., Part II. and the Staff Manual respectively. Title pages will be prepared in manuscript.

Hour, Date, Place	Summary of Events and Information	Remarks and references to Appendices
HEBUTERNE 24 Sept	1 Section of 2nd J.A. Bde under MAJ LATTEY carried out wire cutting position alongside 1st Bty. Morning quiet.	All references are to 1/20000 No 2 dated 15th July 1915.
1.30 a.m.		
2.30 p.m.	2nd Bty cut wire successfully at 663, 120 rounds range 2800. The wire was well enfiladed & was old wire. It was done with a section. The other section bombarded 'S69 & 365 in 3rd line trenches with 100 H.E. 3rd Battery cut wire successfully at 673 with 200 rounds range 2850. The wire was enfiladed & was 1/2 old & 1/2 new. In both these cases a lane was cut clean through.	
4. p.m.	3rd Bty wire cutting at 301. As yesterday old wire cut but little or no impression made on new wire. 200 rounds. Range 2675.	
4.30 p.m.	2nd Bty fired 20 rounds shrapnel at trenches S.W. of L.A. LOUVIERE FARM.	
5 p.m.	2nd Bty fired 12 rounds ∧ in PUISIEUX shrapnel	
5.30 p.m.	2nd Bty co-operating with 4m (How) Bde fired 40 rounds shrapnel on LA LOUVIERE FME.	
11 p.m.	The section of 2nd Bde withdrawn. 1st & 2nd Btys returned to their former positions. During night 14 rounds were fired on working party at 673 and at 663.	2/8

XIV (vi)

Army Form C. 2118.

Instructions regarding War Diaries and Intelligence Summaries are contained in F. S. Regs., Part II. and the Staff Manual respectively. Title pages will be prepared in manuscript.

WAR DIARY
of 1st S.M. Wks R.F.A.
or
INTELLIGENCE SUMMARY.
(Erase heading not required.)

Hour, Date, Place	Summary of Events and Information	Remarks and references to Appendices
HEBUTERNE 25th Sept/15 12 noon	A quiet morning. B.O.C.R.A. inspected 3rd Battery position. 2nd Battery wire cutting. 301. 157 Shrapnel + 25 H.E. The wire at this front is about 100 to 150 yards deep in heavy coils very thick. Patrols report it is (not barbed), 9 to 1 inch thick "some of it as thick as ones little finger"; the wire is undoubtedly cut but the lane does not reach up to the desired point. It will require much more attention. It should be noted that best results on this were reported as being obtained with H.E.	
2.30 pm	3rd Bty completed wire cutting. 673 with 40 Shrapnel + 50 H.E.	S.B.
	1st " Shelled sap-head D63 with 25 H.E.	
3.15 pm	1st Bty shelled Trenches 371 to 368. 15 H.E.	
4.15 pm	3rd " " Point D69. 10 H.E.	
6 pm	3rd " " PUISIEUX 10 Shrapnel + 10 H.E.	
	1st " " LALOUVIERE FARM in conjunction with 96 rounds.	
	10 Shrapnel.	
7.30 pm	3rd Battery moved to the old 1st Battery position	
During night	1st Battery fired 12 Shrapnel at point 673 + 4 at D63	
	2nd " " 12 " " " " 301	
26th Sept/1.15 am	1st " " just 12 rounds into PUISIEUX + 14 into LA LOUVIERE FARM. A quiet day. No aeroplane parties seen.	
5 pm	2nd " fired 10 H.E. at 301. transept with aircless. Practically no hostile fire. 2/Lt E.H. BLAND from 3 w/s joined. Attached to Ammn. Col. S/B	S.B.

XIV. (vii)

Army Form C. 2118.

WAR DIARY
of 1st or North Midland Brigade R.F.A.

INTELLIGENCE SUMMARY.
(Erase heading not required.)

Instructions regarding War Diaries and Intelligence Summaries are contained in F.S. Regs., Part II. and the Staff Manual respectively. Title pages will be prepared in manuscript.

Hour, Date, Place		Summary of Events and Information	Remarks and references to Appendices
HEBUTERNE.	27th Sept 12:15am	Orders received not to fire today at all unless the enemy attacked. Consequently very quiet. Practically no German shelling.	J.B.
	28th Sept	Orders as for 27th. Very quiet practically no German shelling.	J.B.
	29th "	About 2.6 Little Willies on to our trenches & communication trenches during the morning. We did not reply.	J.B.
	30th "	Orders as for 29th to continue until further notice, unless permission obtained from 48th Divn Arty.	
	1pm to 1:20	Heavy bombardment by the whole of our fire, support and communication trenches, some 100 to 150 shells of various sizes coming over. Possibly to find out what has become of our artillery during the last few days. No reply was made.	J.B.

(9 20 6) W 4141—463 100,000 9/14 H W V Forms/C. 2118/10

D 48th Division

Original.   October 1915.

                                    121/
                                    7381

CONFIDENTIAL

WAR DIARY.

OF

1st SOUTH MIDLAND BRIGADE RFA

From Oct. 1st   to   Oct 31st   1915.

VOL VIII

AUBalfour
LT. COLONEL,
COMMANDING.
1st S. MIDLAND F.A. BRIGADE

XV 1

Army Form C. 2118.

WAR DIARY
or
INTELLIGENCE SUMMARY of 1st South Midland Brigade R.F.A

(Erase heading not required.)

Instructions regarding War Diaries and Intelligence Summaries are contained in F.S. Regs., Part II. and the Staff Manual respectively. Title pages will be prepared in manuscript.

Hour, Date, Place		Summary of Events and Information	Remarks and references to Appendices
HEBUTERNE	1st October 1915.	Very quiet all day. Reported that the whole of the wire at Point 863 (K19 b·17) and part of the wire at 873 (K17d 2·6) has been repaired. Capt C.E. BOYCE, R.F.A, who for nearly 4 years has held the post of Adjutant of the Brigade, left to take up duty with the 15th Division	S.S.G. E.H.L.
	2nd Oct	Very quiet. Only 2 shells on our zone.	
	3rd Oct	Heavy mist all morning. Two German working parties seen repairing front line trench. Our guns did not fire. Capt. G.R. BENSON RFA arrived and took up duties as Adjutant	SRM.
	4th Oct.	77 Cm gun dropped 10 shells in HEBUTERNE and 3 shells on 2ND BATTY O.P. at CARRIERE, also 3 shells near CENTRAL. In the afternoon more intermittent GERMAN shelling. Our guns did not fire. GERMAN balloon went up from 2·30 pm till 4·10 pm. Several signs of movement.	SRM.
	5th Oct.	Quiet and misty. A few German rounds on our trenches and HEBUTERNE. Afternoon observation very difficult. About 40 shell on various fronts of our line.	SRM
	6th Oct	Too misty for observation till 8 a.m. 12 rounds on HEBUTERNE from 77 mm gun during the morning, several premature went Observed by O.C. 3rd Batty sun L 25 a 6.3. Intermittent bombardment during afternoon from 77 mm, several not exploding from	SRM

XV 2

Army Form C. 2118.

WAR DIARY
or
INTELLIGENCE SUMMARY. 1/1st South Midland Bde RFA

(Erase heading not required.)

Instructions regarding War Diaries and Intelligence Summaries are contained in F. S. Regs., Part II. and the Staff Manual respectively. Title pages will be prepared in manuscript.

Hour, Date, Place	Summary of Events and Information	Remarks and references to Appendices
HEBUTERNE 7th Oct.	Quiet most all morning. About 20 field gun shells into our line, just before noon. O.C. 2nd Batt'y again spotted discharge from gun, but not good enough to engage to observation. Afternoon a German working party shewn by O.C. 1st Batt'y repairing trench K.17 & 2.7. 4.30 – 5.30 pm German field guns bombarded the 4th Div. on our right, and two shells fell near 2nd Batt'y O.P. A fire was seen in direction of BUCQUOY 9pm.	9pm
8th Oct.	Morning clearer. Two bouquets of 6 field gun shells each, about 8 a.m. near HEBUTERNE and on our right flank. 2.0 p.m. 6 rounds field gun on communication trench just E.of HEBUTERNE) 3.30 – 5 pm. About 40 field gun shells and some French howitzer on support trenches K 28 b.	9pm
9th Oct.	Morning very misty again. Very quiet till afternoon. 12.45 pm – 6 pm. about 10 scattered 77 mm rounds in section H & J. Evening misty.	9pm
10th Oct.	Misty. 11.20 a.m. 20 77mm in K16a communication trench close to HEBUTERNE. 12.30 p.m. 12 77 mm's on fire trenches in section G & H. 1.55 pm. German aeroplane close over 1st Batt'ys O.P. 3 pm. 12 rounds from 105 mm howitzer fell on trench K29c.	9pm
11th Oct.	Clear morning. 6.50 a.m. 3 rounds 77mm into trench 23. 9.40 am. German biplane flying south over our trenches low. 10.50 a few rounds 77 mm on support trenches in K16 b. 11.45 German heavy field gun shot 4 rounds at SAILLY. 3 pm. 8.77 pm HE shells into 2nd Batty O.P. CARRIERE. 7.30 pm German searchlight.	9pm

XV 3

Army Form C. 2118.

WAR DIARY
or
INTELLIGENCE SUMMARY. of 1st South Midland Bde RFA

(Erase heading not required.)

Hour, Date, Place	Summary of Events and Information	Remarks and references to Appendices
HEBUTERNE 12th Oct.	Too misty to observe till 9 a.m. When 3 77mm dropped near CARRIERE. Quiet morning. 1.10 pm — 1.20 pm Germans shelled HEBUTERNE. 2nd Bty. OP at CARRIERE, and trenches. 2.40 Germans aeroplane flying N.NE. Balloon up till 5 pm. 3.45 12 English aeroplanes flew E and set fire to something in ACHIET railway station; at the same time 2nd, 3rd & 4th Brigades carried out an enterprise in direction of GOMMECOURT Wood	from
13th Oct.	Very quiet morning. 11:40 to 2:30 h promiscuous shelling at intervals, to which we replied 3 pm 1st Battery fired at a German working party at K17 b13 with effect. 3.30 to 3.50. German howrs shelled SAILLY and COIGNEUCAMP. Balloon up 4.30 Balloon down. Some further shelling of our communication trenches at 5 pm.	from
14th Oct.	Thick mist. All quiet till 3.45 pm when 1st Battery fired on a working party. Scattered German bombardment. At 6 pm 3 tremendous explosions in the line, but most too thick. Probable aerial torpedoes.	from
15th Oct.	Thick fog all morning till 11.45 am. Mist again all evening. Trench 32 K23 b 73.	from
16th Oct.	Thick fog all morning. Intermittent bombardment of our front trenches began about 2.30 pm. At 2.40 pm the Brigade fired 23 rounds in German trenches about K17 d 21. Gentle retaliation at 4 pm	from
17th Oct.	Fog all morning. At 11.35 am the Brigade fired 27 rounds on our own wire about L14 c 58. North of PUISIEUX. This must have annoyed the Germans as they then proceeded to put about 300 rounds on SAILLY and HEBUTERNE. All calibres, chiefly 5.9"How. 4 men wounded in HEBUTERNE. Reported 3 men killed and many wounded in SAILLY. Our Brigade fired 26 rounds into PUISIEUX, and so did three of our guns, but it did not check bombardment.	from

XV 4

WAR DIARY
or
INTELLIGENCE SUMMARY.
(Erase heading not required.)

Army Form C. 2118.

Instructions regarding War Diaries and Intelligence Summaries are contained in F. S. Regs., Part II. and the Staff Manual respectively. Title pages will be prepared in manuscript.

Hour, Date, Place	Summary of Events and Information	Remarks and references to Appendices
HEBUTERNE. Oct 18th.	9.30 to 10.30 am. Germans shelled HEBUTERNE and Trenches 21 and 32 with heavy howitzers, and 2nd Battery OP with field guns. We fired 12 rounds in support of infantry. 12.15 pm the Germans shelled on Trenches 21, 32, & 34 with minenwerfer, 5.9 Howitzer and 8.2 Howitzer (1st appearance here) about 350 rounds, there and in HEBUTERNE. Trench 32 was completely blotted out, but only one Infantry Officer and one man was killed there, many were wounded. We replied at 3.25 pm with 56 rounds on German front line from K.11 d.20 to K.17 d.4, and in K.23 b. The other Brigades and our Heavies and the infantry cooperated, also an aeroplane. The aeroplane saw hundreds of black objects suggested to be gas cylinders in the German front line stretched to our line. They were few or six feet apart and stretched side by side from GOMMECOURT to BEAUMONT HAMEL. Prepared for gas attack. 2nd Battery kept Germans opposite on ruined Trench 32 (copy) with occasional bursts of fire from 6 pm to 8 pm.	from
Oct 19th.	Quiet all morning. Infantry came out whole today. 144th Brigade replace 145th mostly. In the afternoon the Germans continued bombarding, commenced round Trench 32 with 8.2" Hows and trench mortars about 16 rounds as well as scattering a few field gun shells on our observing station. The 1st Battery at 3.30 pm discovered German Art: Officers quarters in front of Trench K.17 b 1680 and shelled them.	from

(9 29 6) W 4141—463 100,000 9/14 H W V Forms/C. 2118/10

XV S

Army Form C. 2118.

WAR DIARY
or
INTELLIGENCE SUMMARY.
(Erase heading not required.)

Instructions regarding War Diaries and Intelligence Summaries are contained in F.S. Regs., Part II. and the Staff Manual respectively. Title pages will be prepared in manuscript.

Hour, Date, Place		Summary of Events and Information	Remarks and references to Appendices
HERUTERNE	Oct 20th	Thick mist all morning and very quiet. From 12 noon till 2.45 pm Enemy shelled our trenches with about 15 field gun shell, and also 2nd Bty. O.S. with about 40 rounds.	gen.
	Oct 21st	Austrian quiet misty morning. At 1.20 pm Enemy shelled trenches in various parts with about 12 – 77 mm rounds, and 2nd Bty O.S. with about 20 rounds till 3.15 pm.	gen.
	Oct 22nd	Misty morning. A few 77 mm rounds on K27a at 8.10 am. 10 am to 11.30 heavy bombardment of 4th Div Trenches on our right with 5.9"/ and Trench mortars. At 2pm a German B-plane flew over HERUTERNE. From 2 pm to 3.15 pm 18 · 77 mm rounds near Central K216, 2½. At 3.15 1st Bty fired 6 rounds at a working party K186.04 and stopped their work. At 4.45 pm. 2nd Bty fired 5 rds on night line.	gen. gen.
	Oct 23rd	Very misty and quiet till 10 am. 10 to 11·10 am Germans shelled our trenches and Central O.S. with 20 · 77 mm. At 11.45 am a German aeroplane was seen hovering over PUISIEUX. Afternoon 12.30 to 4.15 pm Enemy directed about 50 · 77 mm rounds scattered over various points in our line. At 3.30 pm. we carried out a bombardment arranged by the 1st Division. The 1st Batty fired 40 rds HE on trenches K17 b 29 to K17 b 06. and K17 c 35·25 to K17 d 47. 2nd Battery 20 rds HE on K17 d 41 to K27 b 58. 3rd Bty 40 HE on enemy 2nd line K17 d 41 to K17 d 49. G.O.C Division complimented Brigade on fine shooting. Many direct hits and parapets destroyed	gen.

WAR DIARY
or
INTELLIGENCE SUMMARY.
(Erase heading not required.)

Army Form C. 2118.

Hour, Date, Place	Summary of Events and Information	Remarks and references to Appendices
HEBUTERNE 24th Oct.	Enemy made feeble reply. 3rd Battery spotted a dummy flare battery but was not taken in for long. During the evening we kept up an intermittent fire till midnight on the track which had been broken down. No troops or working parties. Infantry reported that they stopped the work. At 6 am it was quiet and misty. Practically no shooting till 11 am. At 11.15 am 1st Batt fired 7 shrapnel on K.18.a.8.4 and 6 HE on K.17.b.17. 12.5 3rd Batty fired 10 rounds with 2 rounds. At 4.5 pm 4.77 mm fell into HEBUTERNE and 3rd Batt stopped flash heard 96 rm K.21.b.1.2.b. At 10.45 pm 2nd & 3rd Batterys fired at test S.O.S. which was fired quickly and successfully directed the nearest corner. 8 rounds altogether.	from.
25th Oct. 26th Oct.	All quiet and very misty all morning and afternoon. 6 am it was very clear and coming to a heavy wind the clouds had cleared the view considerably. At 9.10 am a German biplane flew back and forth over our lines. At 9.40 2.4.2" HE rounds on or near trench 27, to which 3rd Battery replied by 4 rounds on K.17.a.3.5. The dummy battery near SERRE started again and 3rd Batt1 fired 4 rounds at it. Bombardment of 4th Div Trenches with field guns 9.50 to 10.15 am 12.30 pm 1st Battery fired at working party K.18.62.6. with effect. at 1.30 pm and 4.30 pm About 25 77 mm scattered between 2nd and 3rd Battys O.S.	Gren. from.

WAR DIARY
or
INTELLIGENCE SUMMARY

Army Form C. 2118.

Hour, Date, Place	Summary of Events and Information	Remarks and references to Appendices
HEAUTERNE. Oct 27th	Wet and misty till 8.30 am then cleared. 30 77mm on trench K23c and K22d at 11 am. Retaliated by 7th Bty on firing rounds on what turned out to be a working party at K17 6.74 and K17 6.8.6. Infantry reported good effect. At 11 am the smoke of a train was seen in PUISIEUX going North. At 12 noon it started raining till 1.50 pm. Intermittent and scattered bombardment till 4 pm from 77mm guns about 30 rounds in all. Three Balloons were up in German lines at 2.30 pm and the light was excellent. Bearings 10°, 66° and 110° from K16 c 2.7. Some movement 7 wagons seen in PUISIEUX and BUCQUOY. An English aeroplane made short reconnaissance at 3.20 - 3.40 pm. At 4.30 pm the light was bad and all balloons descended. One flash bath appeared still active.	
Oct 28th	Mist and rain all quiet. Cleared at 10 am but light bad. Intermittent bombardment with 77mm; all morning. 11 am started raining again. Heavy battery still active all afternoon 77mm intermittent on our trenches. Rained all afternoon. At 7.30 pm a German French Mortar about 30 rounds. 3rd Battery retaliated with 12 rounds on nights lines reported effective by Infantry. Opened heavy fire on trench 2.8.	gpen
Oct 29th	6 - 8 am misty 9 to 10 am. Scattered bombardment from 77mm about 20 rounds. At 11 am 2nd Batty fired 7 rounds in a working party K23 697 with good effect.	gpen

XV 8

WAR DIARY
or
INTELLIGENCE SUMMARY.
(Erase heading not required.)

Army Form C. 2118.

Hour, Date, Place	Summary of Events and Information	Remarks and references to Appendices
HÉBUTERNE Oct 30th	Bombardment from 77 mm on various points at 2nd Batty O.S. at 3 pm. Light good. 18 Shrap & 15 HE on Trenches K17 d 41 to K24 a 0 b. 3rd Batty 19 Shrap & 15 HE on support trench K17 b 32 to K17 d 41. 3.10 pm 1st Batty fired 16 Shrap & 20 HE on Trenches K17 b 07 to K17 b 29. 3rd Batty complained of some defective Ammn. At 3.15.15 77 mm arrived in 2nd Batty O.S. no retaliation. Clear morning. 7.30 to 12 mm intermittent bombardment with 77 mm on various points in our line, about 20 rounds. 5 Balloons went up at 10 am, bearings 67°; 14°; 10°; 3°; and 54°; from K16 c 27. Activity & tearful and wanton factor seen far behind German lines. At 9.25 am a British aeroplane was ranging a heavy battery. The German fired no AA guns at it only machine guns. Green seen in ACHIET RLY STN. 12 mm. No. 1259 Bombr J M P PHILLIPS was severely wounded by 77 mm at 2nd Bty O.S. Died at 1.55 pm. 1.30 pm. 1st Batty fired 4 rounds on German observers in Trenches K17 b 27. Intermittent bombardment with 77 mm. 3.50 pm. Two British aeroplanes dropped bombs apparently with success on position in PUISIEUX BUCQUOY road at a working party K18 b 86. 4.0 pm 1st Batty fired 6 rounds. 4.35 pm. Balloon finally descended. View clear.	RW RW 2ndLt RW

XV 9

Army Form C. 2118.

WAR DIARY
or
INTELLIGENCE SUMMARY.
(Erase heading not required.)

Instructions regarding War Diaries and Intelligence Summaries are contained in F.S. Regs., Part II. and the Staff Manual respectively. Title pages will be prepared in manuscript.

Hour, Date, Place	Summary of Events and Information	Remarks and references to Appendices
HERSUTERNE. OCT 31.	Quiet clear morning. 7.45 am. 13 rounds 77 mm on HEBUTERNE close to Bde HQrs. 9 am 3 4.2" shells in town place. 9.20 am 1st Bty fired 2 rounds at 2 snipers at K17 & K13.7. 9.40 am. Rain fell and light became bad. 10.15 am. 1st Batty fired 11 rounds at snipers as before, also at a working party K.18 & 74 with good effect. 2nd Batty fired 15 rounds on two working parties K.2.4 & 9.5. L.19.a.15. who stopped work. 11.30 am. 1st Batty fired 4 rounds at working party K.18.b.74. 12.25 pm to 1.45 pm intermittent firing from 77 mm round about 2nd Bty O.S. At 2 pm 1st Battery fired 6 rounds on to K.17 b. One of their wounded India was picked up in the line and bayoneted an infantry. The fire pretended light from all day.	Snow. A.u. Beefun LtCol RFA

48th Division

ORIGINAL.   November 1915.

CONFIDENTIAL.

WAR DIARY.   121/7694

OF

1st South Midland Brigade R.F.A.

From Nov. 1st.   to   Nov 30th.   1915.

VOLUME ~~XVI~~ IX

AM Balfour
LT. COLONEL,
COMMANDING,
1/1st S. MIDLAND F.A. BRIGADE.

XVI-1

Army Form C. 2118.

WAR DIARY
or
INTELLIGENCE SUMMARY.
(Erase heading not required.)

Instructions regarding War Diaries and Intelligence Summaries are contained in F.S. Regs., Part II. and the Staff Manual respectively. Title pages will be prepared in manuscript.

Hour, Date, Place	Summary of Events and Information	Remarks and references to Appendices
HEBUTERNE. Nov 1st 1915.	Quiet + rain until 10 am. Intermittent bombardment on trenches at K.17 c.6.0, in front of HEBUTERNE + in 4th Division area. Slight lull from 11 am until nightfall. Generals ANSHAWE and ANHENRY, commanding 46th Division + 3rd Army respectively, visited 2nd Howr Battery O.P. at 11.20 am.	GOC.
Nov 2nd.	Raining and windy. Difficult observation all day. During the morning about 40 enemy rounds fell all along our line and at 2nd Battery O.P. At 10 am 2nd Battery stopped an enemy working party in K24 b.t.4. About 1 pm the enemy shelled C.2 H.1 N.6 A.M.P.S. with 8 rounds and also put 12 rounds from H.2 How'r near 2nd Battery Pers Gun at K14 c 8.1.1. Rest of afternoon quiet. Slight very bad.	GOC.
Nov 3rd.	At 8 o'clock quiet. Weather low cloud along our line and we didn't being fired at. About 8.30 the enemy bombarded HEBUTERNE with 85-77 m/m rounds. At 11.30 am the 2nd Bty observed a section of 9 guns coming into action at K19.9.1. and fired 18 rounds with good effect. During the afternoon intermittent bombardment of HEBUTERNE with 77m/m + H.2 How'rs. About 80 rounds in all. 1st + 2nd Batteries fired with success on working parties at K.18 a.1.5.4. and K.34 b.9.9. At 6 o'clock more fell	GOC.

XVI 2

WAR DIARY
or
INTELLIGENCE SUMMARY
(Erase heading not required.)

Army Form C. 2118.

Hour, Date, Place	Summary of Events and Information	Remarks and references to Appendices
HEBUTERNE — Nov 4th 1915	Foggy & quiet morning. Clearing occasionally. Rifle mounted Aeroplane bombarded no C was seen over of our lines. At 12 noon the fog lifted. During the afternoon the enemy fired about 50 rounds at HEBUTERN and Bull Battery O.P. Shortly after 8pm a British Aeroplane carried out a reconnaissance without being fired on. 4.30pm. Priestly General mist until 10am. 10.15 to 10.45 am bombardment of 2nd Battery O.P. with 77mm + 4.2". About 20 rounds. At 11am bombardment C was seen & gully carried out.	
" 5th	1st Battery. — fired 20 Shrap. and 30 H.E. between K11d 4.0 and K17d 2.0 and K17 to 0.3. ditto — 18 Shrap. + 10 H.E. between K11d 4.0 and K17 to 3.2. 2nd Battery. — fired 10 Shrap. + 16 H.E. on K17d 4.1 to K17d 7.2. ditto — 5 Shrap. + 4 H.E. on K24a 0.9. 3rd Battery. — 15 Shrap + 10 HE on K17 8.2 to K17d 4.1. About 35 direct hits were obtained. The Enemy retaliated with again putting 2 6-77/m + 4.2" into 2nd Battery O.P. and about 40-77m or so Female in K&8R. 12.5pm. 3rd Battery fired 6rds on battery in action at K18d 6±8. At 1pm rain obscured the view until 4pm when 3rd Battery registered K12d 4.0. 6rds 4.2" fell on Isolated piece of HEBUTERNE in retaliation. 9.0pm. Very was called on by Infy. + fired 8rds on enemy's line with effect.	

XVI 3

Army Form C. 2118.

WAR DIARY
or
INTELLIGENCE SUMMARY.
(Erase heading not required.)

Instructions regarding War Diaries and Intelligence Summaries are contained in F. S. Regs., Part II. and the Staff Manual respectively. Title pages will be prepared in manuscript.

Hour, Date, Place	Summary of Events and Information	Remarks and references to Appendices
HEBUTERNE Nov 6th 1916.	Heavy fog all day. No firing on either side. Aeroplanes fired/flaring overhead at 2am & 3.30am.	R.W.M
" 7th.	Misty until noon. During the morning the enemy fired about 80 - 77m on 2nd Bty. O.P., our Batteries in SECTOR A & 4th Divisional Area on our right. 12.35 pm. 2nd Battery discovered an Anti-Aircraft section about K.17.a.6.5. and fired 9 rounds. Intermittent German bombardment throughout afternoon on all our Battery O.Ps and HEBUTERNE. Several shells which were reported British Aeroplanes appeared to burst a position E - PUISIEUX and at 3.40 a British Aeroplane appeared to fall at about PUISIEUX Station causing a loud explosion & volume of smoke. Trench fog until 10 am. At 10 am. Several Hostile Anti-Aircraft sections at A.19.d. were engaged by 3rd Battery and 1st Bam 1st Bty fired 8 rounds on K.17.b.2.7. From 12 noon until then intermittent German bombardment making 8 - 5.9" Hows. 1st and 3rd Bty retaliated with 10 rounds into SAILLY.	R.W.M
" 8th.		R.W.M
" 9th.	Mainly until 10 am. Heavy German bombardment from 2am until noon on our observation Station with 77 mm. about 80 rounds, including also 30 heavy howitzer rounds on HEBUTERNE and SAILLY. Our Batteries retaliated with 80 rounds on German front line trench. At 12 noon German fired 12-77 pr on K FOOTVENT FERNIE 1st Bty fired at 3.10 with guns on K.17 & 1½ ems K.17.d.1.8.2.	R.W.M
" 10th.	Clear & quiet morning. 8.15 am. 1st Bty fired 4 rounds fring fartly at K.17.b.1.8 and stopped that work	R.W.M

(D 22 6) W 4141—463 100,000 9/14 H W V Forms/C. 2118/10

XVI 4

WAR DIARY
or
INTELLIGENCE SUMMARY.
(Erase heading not required.)

Army Form C. 2118.

Hour, Date, Place	Summary of Events and Information	Remarks and references to Appendices
HEBUTERNE - Nov 10th 1915	at 3pm enemy shelled HA SIGNY FERME with 77m/m (H.K.S.W. Area) B.4.6 p.m. a British Aeroplane carried out reconnaissance towards N.E., returning without being fired upon. At 10 p.m. 4-5.9" How's fell in 2nd R/y.	A.A.A.
" 11th. -	Clear & Sunny. Quiet morning. Several Aeroplanes on both sides were up. 9 am & 10 am A Sen.t Enemy aeroplanes were heard N. of HEBUTERNE. While Balloon ascended at 10 am inside from Battery positions. During afternoon our batteries registered. The enemy fired about 6-77 m/m Shells at 2nd R/y, O.P. 2nd Battery changed O.P. to CENTRAL (N.v.13.4) Strong working parties (about 60 men) east of road beyond PUISIEUX - BUCQUOY Rd. Out of range. 9 each train seen beyond same road.	A.A.A.
" 12th. -	Steady rain until 2 pm. German and motor transport between CENTRAL and HA SIGNY FERME busy and our Bty registered on working on limbers drawing about 30 rds 77 m/m. Shown in vicinity of CENTRAL. 1st Bty fired at 600 working parties at K1806 & and K190.67½. During afternoon about 12-77 m/m fell at HA SIGNY Light.	A.A.A.
" 13th. -	Light, excellent all day. Germans walking about in parapets were fired on and shot at by our Batteries throughout morning. (about 25 rounds). More rain fell from 1 pm until evening. Our batteries again fired on Germans working on parapets. At 10.30 pm at K17.4.4. 2, with excellent effect.	A.A.A.

WAR DIARY or INTELLIGENCE SUMMARY

Army Form C. 2118.

XVI 5

Hour, Date, Place	Summary of Events and Information	Remarks and references to Appendices

HEBUTERNE Nov 14th 1915

Fine clear morning. 2nd R.F.A. registered points in this Div. area with a view to searching the Sap Rde R.F.A. on enemy's area with a barrage if required. 9.20 am 2nd R.F.A. discovered a steam pump at K17d.6.5. which they put out of action, with 6 shots - 10 H.E. 10am 8 Balloons(enemy) were reported, which prevented our guns from firing until 11.15am when the Balloons were obscured by high clouds. In this we carried out a bombardment. 2nd R.F.A. fired 88 shaps at HAMOUVIERE FERME - trenches in vicinity and 12 H.E. on trenches at point 301 with considerable destructive effect, fires started, first battery fired 18 rounds at LA NOUVERE FERME causing great damage to enemy's works. By way of retaliation the germans fired about 40 rounds 77mm on our trenches in SECTOR H1 and 12.30pm first battery fired 18 rounds at K17b1.7 and 2nd R/4 on old Observation Station. LA CARRIERE. All night long our batteries engaged the damaged parts with short bursts of shrapnel and the Infy reported that enemy's working parties fatigue were heard. In the morning enemy was feeling & light good until 8am when there was a m.g. fire. This lasted until 11.25am. Ordinaries & 9am when light was again good. 3rd R/F at 8 and 11.25am continued working parties at K17b9.0 and K9d4.9.5 Investigation   Rec
Secure opened and we continued firing with difficulty until 10PM   Rec

Further firing was continued on the chief points in the sector by our batteries.

November 15th

Form/C. 2118/15

XVI 6.

Army Form C. 2118.

WAR DIARY
or
INTELLIGENCE SUMMARY.
(Erase heading not required.)

Hour, Date, Place	Summary of Events and Information	Remarks and references to Appendices
HEBUTERNE Nov 15th	12 noon to 1 pm. 4 et majors bombarded HEBUTERNE & CARRIERE with 30 rounds, 77m pt. 2, 3. In retaliation 1st Rty bombarded K182.a.7.5. with 10 rounds. 1 pm. 2nd & 3rd Btties engaged two Anti-Aircraft guns about 4.9d. 6.5. which were seen to put up shields and move off S.E. Allthough platoons which was this released military put up Germans were unsatisfactory stationing in the open and made engagement with our aero planes at 2.30 to 3 pm and at 4.30 pm at which times Balloons up. Traffic ration parties were seen in 4.9d at 8.15 pm.	FJM
" 16th	Snow was on the ground slight frost but observation & chrapnel very difficult. Our Batteries continued their harrassing tactics, evidently causing great annoyance. They stopped the jumping German trench scared a number shooting far the 15 gun for cover, dropping their tools. Our men became more cautious, jumping down into the flooded trench, whenever they heard an shell coming. Smokes from them. Light pails improving. 8.30 am - 8-5-9.3 fell on our trenches 23 + 24, were at once replaced 15 by 1st Rty firing 16 rounds at K.19d. 6.5. 9 am. 10.4.2 on HA CARRIERES. 11.5 am 2nd + 3rd Batteries engaged strong working party at K17d 9.9 am silenced an Anti-Aircraft station at K.19d. 6.6. New advance post x ens cluderunt 1.30 pm. During afternoon the German put about 20 rounds into CARRIERE and our trenches 23, 24, 27 and 28. 1st + 3rd Rty, not battled on wood 872, HA HOUIERE FERME 15 rounds on Hun K.17.18. This stopped enemy firing. and German trenches K.17.18.	FJM
" 17th		FJM

XVI.7.

WAR DIARY
or
INTELLIGENCE SUMMARY.
(Erase heading not required.)

Army Form C. 2118.

Instructions regarding War Diaries and Intelligence Summaries are contained in F.S. Regs., Part II. and the Staff Manual respectively. Title pages will be prepared in manuscript.

Hour, Date, Place	Summary of Events and Information	Remarks and references to Appendices
HEBUTERNE Nov 18th 1915	6.20 a.m. Very misty. German machine guns active N. HEBUTERNE. 7.45 a.m. Light bombardment of 4th Divl. front. 8.40 a.m. Enemy formation from Sq.4, 1st Bty dispersed working party K17 c.9.? Foggy all day. 3.10 p.m. 1st Bty dispersed about 65 [?] cattle on our right. trenches. At 7.30 p.m. 1st & 3rd Btys retaliated with 12 Shrap + 8 H.E. on night relief.	JRW
" 19th "	Thick fog. German infantry invisible all day. 4 - 4.20 pm 10 rounds on LA CARRIERE, TOUTVENT FERME and K23a. trenches. 3rd Bty retaliated with 32 Shrap. and 6 HE into wood K72 + K19 A.3.7.	JRW
" 20th "	Dark but clear morning. Intermittent bombardment of HEBUTERNE. CARRIERE and 4th Divl. trenches SECTOR H. throughout morning. 9.50 am Germans observed working near LA HOOVERE. During afternoon about 60 Trench Mortar rounds on CENTRAL CARRIERE & SECTOR H.	JRW
" 21st "	Thick fog until 8.30 am. Intermittent bombardment of front trenches and 4th Division area from 10 until 11 a.m. 10 am 3rd Battery fired 4 rounds on a gun at LA HOOVERE and 12 pbs. on trenades K.24.5.8. 10.30 am 3rd Bty fired 4 H.E. on K24.c.3.9 in retaliation. 10.50 am 1st Bty also retaliated with 8 Shrap. on K18 B.0.7.1. Light rain generally all day. 10.15 pm. 3rd Bty. dispersed working party at K roadings K.23.b.2.9 keeping their guns laid on this point.	JRW
" 22nd "	12.50 a.m.- 30+R. was again resumed at K23.b.29 and again stopped by 3rd Battery. 12.30 to 6 am. Bombardment by enemy of our right trenches at 4th Division area. Thick fog the whole of the day. No firing.	JRW
" 23rd "	Thick fog until noon. 1.5 pm. Bombardment of CENTRAL, ETONIAN 2nd & 3rd Bty. retaliated with 16 rounds on HA HOOVIERE and K24 a.b.9. which silenced enemy's fire.	JRW

Forms/C.2118/14. (9 29 6) W 4141—463 100,000 9/14 H W V

XVI-8.

WAR DIARY
or
INTELLIGENCE SUMMARY.
(Erase heading not required.)

Army Form C. 2118.

1915

Hour, Date, Place	Summary of Events and Information	Remarks and references to Appendices
HEBUTERNE 23rd.	3 am. 2nd Bty. dispersed a working party reported by Infy at K.20.a.7.6. Our Infy reported some Germans carried away on stretchers. Again at 6 pm. they fired on this point with success. Clear morning. 8.30 am to 9 am. Heavy bombardment of trenches near TOUTVENT FARM and to the N of it by Div. Arty. with about 100 rounds mostly 4.5" how. interspersed with a few 18 pdrs. & some 60prs firing at 6.8". 9 am to 11.30 am intermittent bombardment of German Starving Stations. Several blind shells observed. 3rd Bty. retaliated at 9.5 on HANOUVIERE, and at 11.15 on wood L.13.d.2.6. 1.15 pm 1st Bty. dispersed working party K.18.a.7.5. 3.35 pm. 1st Bty. destroyed an Observation Post reported by Infy at K.17.d.1.6 with 19 rounds.	fired.
24th.	Misty until 9am. 6.30 to 7am. At. regist. and aeroplane aeroplane. 2nd + 3rd Bty. fired 30 rounds at HANOUVIERE wood L.13.d.0.5 and L.19.a.0.6. The enemy immediately lighted two magnesium flares and K.17.d.5.7 retaliated about a front-line trench with 5 rounds 77m/m. 8am. Light in improved. 8 British aeroplanes flew E. over HEBUTERNE and were fired on by Anti-aircraft guns which flanked appeared on H.19.d. and L.21.d. 11.5 am. 12 lots of rounds on CARRIERE 3rd Bty. retaliated on trench K.17.d.6.5. 11.55 am. W. Bty. carried out aeroplane ranging practice successfully. 12 noon until 3.30 pm about 12.27pm on our trenches in SECTOR H. 2.40 pm. 1st Bty fired 50 Shrapt + 30 H.E. on German trenches in K.17.d. under instructions from W.Bty. Airy Arty. 6pm. 3rd Bty damaged a Machine Gun emplacement at K.23.b.2.9 at request of Infy. following this up with 5 rounds shrapnel as it was being repaired at 12.45 am.	fired.
25th.		###
26th.	During the night some of our batteries to the N. adjusted to form a barrage in direction of GOMMECOURT, to which enemy replied with a few rounds on Eastern outskirts of HEBUTERNE. In the morning we heard of an successful enterprise by 6th Glos. who had entered	fired.

Forms/C. 2118/10

XVI. 9

WAR DIARY
INTELLIGENCE SUMMARY

Army Form C. 2118.

Hour, Date, Place	Summary of Events and Information	Remarks and references to Appendices
HEBUTERNE Nov. 26th.	German working parties in GOMMECOURT Wood bombing & taking ammunition. Aeroplane returning with few casualties. Clear morning. 10.55 am 1st Bty dispersed working party at K18d 7.2. 11 am to 11.40 am 19 rounds 77m on our trenches in K23a. 11.30 am 2nd Bty cancels damaged two machine gun emplacements at K19d 7.2. and K28d 7.9 with 2.9 pdr. 1 pm to 4 pm. Several shrapnel shells into HEBUTERNE. 1.30 pm to 1.40 pm. Sharp fall of snow. 3 pm to 4.30 pm. Light - run eventually good after which sudden fog rendered observation impossible.	FM
27th.	Cloudy morning. 7.10 am. 6-77m fell close to no. Bty O.P. 8.45 am. 15 9.15 am. 2nd & 3rd Bty. dispersed labour parties on [farms] in K17 [?] working in 4.19 a. 1.70a bK 24 + 9.6. 9.30 am Infy reported German firing gun K30.6/32.63 fired on by 3rd Bty. [scrub] bombardment of HEBUTERNE 12.15 pm. 1st Bty dispersed working party K18d 7.2. 1.50 pm to 2.30 pm. About 50 heavy shells fell on the Eastern outskirts of HEBUTERNE. 2.30 pm to 4.0 pm. Two German balloons up. Intermittent bombardment of HEBUTERNE and CARRIERE, replied to by 2nd & 3rd Batteries. 4.5 pm. 1st Bty dispersed working party at K16a 6.5.	FM
28th.	1 am to 1.20 am. Heavy bombardment of HEBUTERNE with Howitzers, Field Machine Gun principally N.E. corner of village. Grenade fell in Brigade Headquarters ditch. Morning clear what fine. 9.30 am. A large German aeroplane with double fuselage flew W. over HEBUTERNE returning at 10 am. Shortly engaged between by our Anti-aircraft guns. 10.30/15 11.30 am about 30 rounds 77m fell around 3rd Bty. (Several blind). 1.30 4 pm. Balloon up. 10.30 pm. 3rd Bty dispersed working party reported by Infy in K23b 2.9.	FM

Forms/C. 2118/10

XVI 10

Army Form C. 2118.

WAR DIARY
or
INTELLIGENCE SUMMARY.
(Erase heading not required.)

Hour, Date, Place	Summary of Events and Information	Remarks and references to Appendices
HEBUTERNE. Nov.29th 1915.	Rainy morning. Slight frost. 10.5am. Enemy began bombardment of our front & reserve trenches which were stopped by 2nd & 3rd Bty firing 6 rounds into wood K.27.b.8.9 in retaliation. 2pm. Heavy rain fell. returned snow. 3pm to 4pm. 1st Bty fired at various points in K.17.b at request of Infy in connection with a patrol reconnaissance. 7.45pm. 2nd Bty dispersed working party reported by Infy at K.9.b.2.8.	SOM.
30th.	Clear morning. 7.50am 1st Bty dispersed working party K.9.b.7.2. 8.45am. 4 British Rifles flew over PUISIEUX, hotly engaged by German Anti-Aircraft guns, a section of which was in turn engaged & silenced by 3rd Bty. 8.55am. One of our planes came back apparently hit. 11.45am. 1st Bty dispersed German ration party who dropped rations & fled. 3pm to 4pm. Many parties of Germans in the open and on SERRE-PUISIEUX road were successfully engaged including an Ambulance cart which was after a shell burst in front of him fell thro' the ditch. 4.35pm. 3rd Bty. repeated ambulance movement & 3 of 9 in communication trench K.17.d.1/2.9 and 1.4.1.5. Bty fired 8 rounds on this points. Throughout the month the relative positions of troops was as follows.—	SOM. SOM.

AwBurton
LT. COLONEL,
COMMANDING
SOM. 1/1st S. MIDLAND F.A. BRIGADE.

```
     143 Inf Bde          144 INF BDE              10th Inf Bde
                        relieved by 145 Bde
      2nd SM                4th/1st     1st SM Bde           29th BDE
      Bde RFA               How          RFA                  RFA
              3 SM BDE
              RFA
         48th DIVISION                              4th DIVISION
```

Original.   December 1915

CONFIDENTIAL.

WAR DIARY

OF

1st SOUTH MIDLAND BRIGADE RFA

From Dec. 1st. to Dec. 31st. 1915.

VOLUME X ~~XVII.~~

A.M. Balfour
LT. COLONEL,
COMMANDING.
1/1st S. MIDLAND F.A. BRIGADE

XVII

Army Form C. 2118.

Instructions regarding War Diaries and Intelligence Summaries are contained in F. S. Regs., Part II. and the Staff Manual respectively. Title pages will be prepared in manuscript.

WAR DIARY
or
INTELLIGENCE SUMMARY.
(Erase heading not required.)

Hour, Date, Place	Summary of Events and Information	Remarks and references to Appendices
HEBUTERNE 1st Decr. 1915	Clear. Enemy appear to be baling their fire trench & K.23.D. Several parties seen walking on the SERRE PUISIEUX Road.	9am
Decr 2nd	Light rain all day & heavy rain. Enemy appear to have strengthened their time in front of trench R.24 B.99.29.1 during last two days.	9am
Decr 3rd	Observation impossible until 1.25 P.M. owing to mist. Prearranged bombardment of enemy; carried out at 1.55 P.M. Retaliation more vigorous than usual — chiefly in HEBUTERNE & trenches east of HEBUTERNE.	9am
Decr 4th 1.35 P.M.	Bombardment with Rifle Grenades of trenches held by the Hun. on our right. Enemy appear to be bathing various portions of their line.	9pm
Decr 5th	2nd Battery fired 150 rounds — were cutting at K.17.D.2.2. with a detached section. The wind was 22-25 yds deep, & a range of 10 or 15 yds appears to have been cut. Even range 1950 yards. At 12.30 P.M. 10 large Howitzer rounds fell in HEBUTERNE. 3rd Battery retaliated on PUISIEUX with 18 H.E. 9.2 Shrapnel. At 4.15 the enemy bombarded SAILLY heavily. 1st Battery retaliated on PUISIEUX with 16 rounds.	9am
Decr 6th	Dull & quiet & light wind. Considerable amount of traffic was seen on the BUCQUOY – PUISIEUX & PUISIEUX – SERRE Roads.	9am

XVII 2.

Army Form C. 2118.

WAR DIARY
or
INTELLIGENCE SUMMARY.
(Erase heading not required.)

Instructions regarding War Diaries and Intelligence Summaries are contained in F.S. Regs., Part II. and the Staff Manual respectively. Title pages will be prepared in manuscript.

Hour, Date, Place	Summary of Events and Information	Remarks and references to Appendices
HEBUTERNE. 7th Dec 1915.	A number of field gun shells fell on our trenches during the morning. 6 in the afternoon the 4th Bn. trenches on our right were bombarded. Rain fell during the afternoon & inspected wind diminished.	pm.
Dec 8th	A number of 7.7 m/m shells on HEBUTERNE during the morning & at 4.20 HEBUTERNE, SAILLY, & COLINCAMPS were shelled. Several flashes were observed. At 4.30 P.M we retaliated on PUISIEUX with 28 rounds - shortly silenced.	pm.
Dec. 9th	From 8.10 to 9.10a HEBUTERNE, SAILLY, & COLINCAMPS were heavily bombarded. No flashes were seen owing probably to the thick mist.	pm.
Dec. 10th	During the morning several rounds in neighbourhood of 1st & 3rd Battery positions. At 3.5 P.M 22 4.2 Howitzer shells in the neighbourhood of La Signy Farm. Raining most of the day. All quiet.	pm. pm.
Dec. 11th		
Dec. 12th	24 heavy Howitzer rounds on the west edge of HEBUTERNE. Light good. At 12.50 P.M the 3rd Battery silenced an Anti-Aircraft Gun at L20 C5.8.	pm. pm.
Dec. 13th	Large German Biplane with double fuselage flew over HEBUTERNE. Light good.	pm
Dec 14th	Intermittent shelling & Communication Trenches throughout the day. (Infantry Relief)	Mell

XVII 3.

Army Form C. 2118.

WAR DIARY
or
INTELLIGENCE SUMMARY.
(Erase heading not required.)

Instructions regarding War Diaries and Intelligence Summaries are contained in F.S. Regs., Part II. and the Staff Manual respectively. Title pages will be prepared in manuscript.

Hour, Date, Place	Summary of Events and Information	Remarks and references to Appendices
HEBUTERNE. 15th Decr 1915.	12 o'clock (Noon). Bombardment of SAILLY HEBUTERNE & 4th Bri. trenches. We retaliated with 21 Shrapnel & 20 H.E. into PUISIEUX, + 10 Shrapnel on Communication Trench to JOUVIERE Farm. At 4.20 PM about 100 shells into SAILLY + 20 into COLINCAMPS. At 4.20 PM WR.M 15 AM from 9nd line adjoining the Brigade. Shells were fired at intervals on various important points in the Enemies lines.	
Dec. 16th	do.	
Dec. 17th	do.	
Dec. 18th	do.	
Dec. 19th	Clear. Intermittent shelling from both sides during the day.	
Dec. 20th	Heavy mist all day. Intermittent shelling from both sides.	
Dec. 21st	do.	
Dec. 22nd	do.	
Dec. 23rd	Clear. Enemy's hostile Artillery rather more active than usual.	
Dec. 24th	All quiet.	
Dec. 25th	(Christmas Day) Enemy opened fire at 7.55 A.M with 5 rounds. The 1st Battery retaliated. No desire to fraternize was shown by the enemy. Continual shelling all day. At 1.15 to 2 P.M. 14 rounds into COLINCAMPS. At 3.20 12 77mm into HEBUTERNE at 3.50 PM 5 rounds into SAILLY. At 4.30 PM bombardment of SAILLY.	

XVII 4.

Army Form C. 2118.

WAR DIARY
or
INTELLIGENCE SUMMARY.
(Erase heading not required.)

Instructions regarding War Diaries and Intelligence Summaries are contained in F.S. Regs., Part II. and the Staff Manual respectively. Title pages will be prepared in manuscript.

Hour, Date, Place	Summary of Events and Information	Remarks and references to Appendices
HEBUTERNE.		
25th Dec. 1915		
Cont.		
Dec. 26th	Numerous flares were observed. At 5.20 we retaliated on PUISIEUX with 15 Shrapnel & 5 H.E.	JM
Dec. 27th	Heavy rain & wind. Observation fairly good. All quiet. Artillery on both sides active throughout the afternoon.	JM
Dec. 28th	Intermittent shelling. Our trenches during the day.	JM
Dec. 29th	At 12.45 A.M. bombardment on 4th Div. trenches by French Mortars & Field Guns. At 2.20.15 77 mm into HEBUTERNE. T.R. 4.2.5. The 2nd Battery retaliated with 20 Shrapnel on SERRE.	JM
Dec. 30th	Heavy mist all day. Intermittent shelling from both sides.	JM
Dec. 31st	12 o'clock (Noon) to 1.10 P.M. prearranged bombardment of German 1st 2nd & 3rd line trenches. 2nd Battery with detached section fired 100 Shrapnel, cutting wire at K.17.B.3.5. The wire was thick & a complete lane was not cut. The enemy retaliated on our trenches & in neighbourhood of 1st & 3rd Battery positions. Throughout the tour the [144th Inf/Bgde] returned by the [142nd] Inf/Bgde. On their right the 18th Bgde (6th Div). The left 143rd Bgde (48th Div). Th	JM

XVII 5.

Army Form C. 2118.

WAR DIARY
or
INTELLIGENCE SUMMARY.
(Erase heading not required.)

Instructions regarding War Diaries and Intelligence Summaries are contained in F. S. Regs., Part II. and the Staff Manual respectively. Title pages will be prepared in manuscript.

Hour, Date, Place	Summary of Events and Information	Remarks and references to Appendices
HEBUTERNE.	The Germans welcomed the New Year at 11 P.M. which is midnight in German time by a hot fusilade during which the Brigade suffered a casualty of one slightly wounded.	

AuBatten
Lt. Colonel
Comdg.
1/1st N. MIDLAND F.A. BRIGADE

ORIGINAL.

CONFIDENTIAL

WAR DIARY

OF

1st SOUTH MIDLAND BRIGADE RFA.

From Jan 1st   to   Jan 31st 1916.

VOLUME ~~XXXXI~~ XI.

Army Form C. 2118

WAR DIARY
or
INTELLIGENCE SUMMARY
(Erase heading not required.)

XVIII (1)

Instructions regarding War Diaries and Intelligence Summaries are contained in F. S. Regs., Part II. and the Staff Manual respectively. Title Pages will be prepared in manuscript.

Place	Date	Hour	Summary of Events and Information	Remarks and references to Appendices
HEBUTERNE	Jan. 1st 1916		Hostile Artillery Field Guns & Howitzers active in afternoon. A number of rounds fell in SAILLY about 4 P.M.	—
"	2nd		All quiet.	—
"	3rd		Several parties of Gunners seen on the SERRE – PUISIEUX Road & fired at. From 1:30 to 3:15 P.M. the enemy heavily bombarded trenches in section "H" & a position of section "S".	—
"	4th		Misty all day.	—
"	5th		Hostile Artillery inactive. A number of rifle-grenades fired into our trenches from K.23.B.2.7	—
"	6th		Foggy most all day.	—
"	7th		A few rounds fell in HEBUTERNE at 9:15 A.M. At 1:30 P.M. 3rd Bty. fired 150 rounds at enemy's wire. The enemy replied with 40 to 50 rounds on our trenches.	—
"	8th		In the morning about a dozen rounds fell in HEBUTERNE. We retaliated on SERRE. The enemy bombarded SAILLY at 12:15 P.M., at 2:10 P.M. & from 3 to 3:30 P.M. On each occasion we replied on PUISIEUX. During the afternoon we carried out a prearranged bombardment of the enemy's trenches & in the course of the bombardment fire broke out north of LOUVIERE Farm, apparently from a rocket or bomb store.	—
"	9th		Quiet day.	—
"	10th		The trenches held by the Div. on our right bombarded at 4:30 P.M.	—
"	11th		Several small parties observed on the PUISIEUX – BUCQUOY Road.	—
"	12th		The enemy apparently constructed a new trench during the night in front of their firing line south of the 16 Poplars extending north round for about 50 yds.	—

1875. Wt. W593/826 1,000,000 4/15 J.B.C. & A. A.D.S.S./Forms/C. 2118.

Army Form C. 2118

WAR DIARY
or
INTELLIGENCE SUMMARY
(Erase heading not required.)

XVIII. (2)

Instructions regarding War Diaries and Intelligence Summaries are contained in F.S. Regs., Part II. and the Staff Manual respectively. Title Pages will be prepared in manuscript.

Place	Date	Hour	Summary of Events and Information	Remarks and references to Appendices
HEBUTERNE	Jan. 13th 1916		Increase in Hostile Rifle-Grenade fire during the afternoon to which we replied on two or three occasions.	pm.
"	14th	"	About a dozen rounds fell in SAILLY at 3.50 P.M. We replied with 2" shrapnel into PUISIEUX.	pm.
"	15th	"	8 77m shells fell near the 3rd Bty. position at 12.25 P.M. During the afternoon we dispersed several working parties on the German 2nd & 3rd lines.	pm.
"	16th	"	Intermittent shelling from both sides during the day.	pm.
"	17th	"	A number of allied aeroplanes (from 25-30) flew west from PUISIEUX about 10.30 A.M. Several rounds fell in HEBUTERNE during the afternoon. We replied by firing into SERRE.	pm.
"	19th	"	Several rounds on HEBUTERNE during the afternoon. We replied on SERRE. About 24 Howitzer shells were fired at the SAILLY-HEBUTERNE Road from 1 to 2 P.M.	pm.
"	19th	"	Intermittent shelling during the day.	pm.
"	20th	"	do	pm.
"	21st	"	do	pm.
"	"	"	We obtained several direct hits on a dugout in the enemies front line trench R.19.B.2.0 The 4th Div. trenches were bombarded with 4.2 Howitzers at 9.30 P.M.	pm.
"	22nd	"	1st Bty. dispersed a rifle-grenade party at 9.45 P.M. At 2.30 to 3 P.M about 50 field-gun shells fired on our trenches in sections G & H in reply to bombardment from our field & heavy guns.	pm.
"	23rd	"	Heavy fog all day.	pm.
"	24th	"	do.	pm.

XVIII (3)

Army Form C. 2118

WAR DIARY
or
INTELLIGENCE SUMMARY
(Erase heading not required.)

Instructions regarding War Diaries and Intelligence Summaries are contained in F. S. Regs., Part II. and the Staff Manual respectively. Title Pages will be prepared in manuscript.

Place	Date	Hour	Summary of Events and Information	Remarks and references to Appendices
HEBUTERNE	Jan. 25th /16		From 2 to 2.30 A.M. bombardment of our trenches north of HEBUTERNE. Several flashes were observed. At 11.35 P.M. a number of hostile aeroplanes passed over HEBUTERNE flying S.W.	from.
	26th		— two being of the Taube type.	from
	27th		Intermittent shelling only. At 7.20 P.M. we received a "Gas alarm" from Infantry, & a barrage was effected on our right line as a precautionary measure. This barrage was subsequently stopped on receipt of orders from the 49th Div. Artillery H.Q. As this gun did not materialize	
	28th		Trenches observed most of the day by mist.	from
	29th		Several working parties were dispersed during the afternoon.	from.
	30th		At 4.3 A.M. we opened a prearranged barrage at 3 points on the enemy's lines to assist Infantry enterprise. Bombs were thrown into the enemies trenches. Several working parties dispersed in the afternoon.	from
	31st		Trenches obscured most of the day by mist. Usual intermittent shelling only.	from.

During the month the following honours were given to the Brigade
Mentioned in dispatches. LT COL A.M. BALFOUR.
                                        MAJ. C.W TODD.
                                        LT W. O. RYAN.
                                        LT E. L. GEDYE

XVIII. (4)

WAR DIARY
or
INTELLIGENCE SUMMARY

Army Form C. 2118

Place	Date	Hour	Summary of Events and Information	Remarks and references to Appendices
			Granted the military cross. LT W. O. RYAN.	
			N.C.Os & men mentioned in dispatches.	
			Corpl. LINGARD. (Bde H.Q.)	
			a/Sjr. DARE (2nd Battz.)	
			Gnr. POWELL (1st Batt.)	
			Dvr. FOOTE. (2nd Battery)	
			N.C.Os & men granted the DCM. Corpl LINGARD	from
			932 DARE.	
			During the whole of the month we supported the 144th INF BDE relieved	
			by 145th INF BDE. On our left, the 143rd INF BDE supported by	
			3rd S.M. Bde RFA. On our right, the 10th INF BDE of the 4th DIVISION,	from
			supported by the 29th Bde RFA.	

Hilliard Major
for LT. COLONEL,
COMMANDING,
1/1st S. MIDLAND F.A. BRIGADE.

Original

CONFIDENTIAL

WAR DIARY

of

1/1st SOUTH MIDLAND BRIGADE. R.F.A.

FROM. FEB. 1st. to FEB. 29th. 1916.

VOLUME. ~~XIX~~ XII

A.H. Beaufort

LT. COLONEL
COMMANDING
1/1st S. MIDLAND R.A. BRIGADE

Army Form C. 2118

WAR DIARY
or
INTELLIGENCE SUMMARY
(Erase heading not required.)

X/4 1.

Instructions regarding War Diaries and Intelligence Summaries are contained in F.S. Regs., Part II. and the Staff Manual respectively. Title Pages will be prepared in manuscript.

Place	Date	Hour	Summary of Events and Information	Remarks and references to Appendices
HEBUTERNE.	Feb. 1st 1916		A few rounds fell on our trenches during the afternoon. Weather fair. All quiet.	JRM
"	2nd		During the afternoon the enemy fired about 100 rounds on our trenches in front of HEBUTERNE. We replied on their front line trenches.	JRM
"	3rd		All quiet. A few rounds were directed on Curiès by the enemy.	JRM
"	4th		At 2:30 we carried out a pre-arranged bombardment of the enemy's rifle & communication trenches. The enemy replied feebly with about 20 rounds on the Brigaderie.	JRM
"	5th		At 4:30 P.M. the enemy shelled HEBUTERNE & La SIGNY FARM. We replied on SERRE.	JRM
"	6th		Intermittent shelling by the enemy. During the day we dispersed several working parties.	JRM
"	7th		Enemy's artillery more active than usual - shells falling on Curiès & our front trenches. We replied on SERRE by request of the Infantry.	JRM
"	8th		Increased shelling by the enemy on HEBUTERNE, Trenches & our Gun positions. We replied on SERRE & their front line trenches.	JRM
"	9th		The enemy shelled HEBUTERNE with a few rounds of H.E. in reply to our bombardment of La LOUVIERE FARM.	JRM
"	10th		Enemy's artillery still active - shells falling in HEBUTERNE, COLINCAMPS, our trenches & SAILLY. We replied by bombarding PUISIEUX.	JRM
"	11th		Enemy's artillery again active - their attention chiefly directed on our front line trenches.	JRM

Army Form C. 2118

WAR DIARY
or
INTELLIGENCE SUMMARY
(Erase heading not required.)

Instructions regarding War Diaries and Intelligence Summaries are contained in F. S. Regs., Part II and the Staff Manual respectively. Title Pages will be prepared in manuscript.

XIX P.

Place	Date	Hour	Summary of Events and Information	Remarks and references to Appendices
HEBUTERNE	Feb. 12th	1916	Intermittent shelling during the day.	
"	13th	"	do do Enemy aeroplanes were driven back by our Anti-Air-Craft Guns & fighting planes.	
"	14th	"	We carried out a pre-arranged bombardment on GOMMECOURT & La LOUVIERE FARM. The enemy replied on our 1st Battery position.	
"	15th	"	Hostile artillery inactive. We dispersed several working parties.	
"	16th	"	A screen was started on the SERRE-PUISIEUX Road. Germans were observed baling water from their trenches — these men appeared to be old, several having grey hair.	
"	17th	"	Heavy transport was observed in the direction of BUCQUOY. During the night a heavy bombardment was directed on HEBUTERNE.	
"	18th	"	Raining & misty — observation not possible. All quiet.	
"	19th	"	Enemy bombarded our front line trenches. Raining & misty.	
"	20th	"	During the afternoon the enemy fired a few rounds on various parts of our trenches north of HEBUTERNE. Observation rather difficult.	
"	21st	"	All quiet. Situation normal.	
"	22nd	"	Snow fell during the afternoon. Hostile lines invisible. All quiet.	
"	23rd	"	Snowing. Observation impossible. All quiet.	
"	24th	"	Situation normal. Further fall of snow.	

XIX 3

Army Form C. 2118

WAR DIARY
or
INTELLIGENCE SUMMARY
(Erase heading not required.)

Instructions regarding War Diaries and Intelligence Summaries are contained in F.S. Regs., Part II. and the Staff Manual respectively. Title Pages will be prepared in manuscript.

Place	Date	Hour	Summary of Events and Information	Remarks and references to Appendices
HEBUTERNE	Feb. 25th 1916		Heavy snowfall during the afternoon. Observation impossible. No artillery fire on either side.	App.
	26th	"	Weather clearing slightly. Little shelling on either side.	App.
	27th	"	Situation normal. During the night a search-light was used by the enemy from SERRE.	App.
	28th	"	Situation normal. All quiet.	App.
	29th	"	Enemy's minenwerfer active during the day. Several working parties were dispersed by our fire & minenwerfer was shelled with H.E.	App.
HEBUTERNE	Feb 9th 1916		Lt. E.V. Sullivan RAMC. & 2nd Lt. G.E.D.E. R.F.A. T.F. joined this Brigade. Capt D.E. FINLAY RAMC.	
	13 1916		2/Lt PTN. TYRRELL + 2 Lt. C.F. HURNDALL joined this Brigade. Left this Brigade.	
			Dispositions. During the month we supported the 145 Bde on our Right the 12th Inf Bde supported by 29th 6th R.F.A. on our left the no 3 Bde supported by the 3 and 6m 8 a R.F.A	App.

Au Beelynn
LT. COLONEL
COMMANDING
158th H. HIGHLAND F.A. BRIGADE

4/3/1916

SECRET

Original

CONFIDENTIAL

War Diary

of

1/1st South Midland Brigade R.F.A.

From March 1st to March 31st 1916

Volume XX

[signature]

LIEUT. COLONEL, R.F.A.
COMMANDING
240th (S.M.) BDE. R.F.A.

WAR DIARY
or
INTELLIGENCE SUMMARY
(Erase heading not required.)

Army Form C. 2118

Place	Date	Hour	Summary of Events and Information	Remarks and references to Appendices
HEBUTERNE	March 1st 1916		Hostile artillery inactive. We dispersed 2 working parties. The day was fine.	AAA
	2nd		Situation quiet. A few hostile shells were fired at our trenches. Raining.	AAA
	3rd		HEBUTERNE was shelled by the Enemy, we took up this trench.	AAA
	4th		Situation normal. A section of our Battery took up new position at COLINCAMPS	AAA
	5th		All quiet. This Brigade moved to COLINCAMPS and took over from the 29th BR MA	AAA
	6th		The 7th WEST RIDING BATTERY was attached to us temporarily	AAA
	7th		Hostile artillery inactive. Our Batteries registered new zones and improved gun pits.	AAA
	8th		During the night the Enemy heavily bombarded trenches to the South. Their aeroplanes were active on our front. Weather fine.	AAA
	9th		Intermittent shelling on both sides during the night. Hostile Aeroplanes active. MINNENWERFERS active during the day. Hostile Artillery inactive. Situation normal.	AAA
	10th		There was minenwerfer shelling on our front orders. Enemy MINNENWERFERS were silenced by our 2nd Battery. Enemy enemy was to fire and ammunition was supplied.	AAA
	11th		Situation normal. Two enemy planes very little shelling observed shelling by enemy. A Battery was ranged by Aeroplane and knocked out no. 3rd Battery position occupied by 3rd Wanwick Battery & received	AAA
	12th		desultory shelling by enemy. Day being shelling during the day. Situation normal. Weather fine.	AAA
	13th		Our fire plans were brought down behind SERRE in train 1 no 3rd Battery. OP. We fired to prevent approach of enemy parties. 4 to 6 pm also fired to break up machine. Col Sullivan Director Wagon Lines and receive division to	AAA
	14th		[illegible] was been attached. to undertaken observation at our Battery armed by [illegible]	AAA

WAR DIARY or INTELLIGENCE SUMMARY

Army Form C. 2118

Place	Date	Hour	Summary of Events and Information	Remarks and references to Appendices
COLINCAMPS	15th 1916		A. & G.O.M. was last at this H.Q. to try B.S.M. Irwin. Amounts to Col. Sherwin guilt. a certain amount of shelling took place in sixth sector. Wants fire and shall	AJL
	16th		An eleven 7 GAS was raised by our front to be German. All quiet normal.	AJL
	17th		Situation normal. In reply to a small bombardment of our trenches we fired 100 rounds into their front lines. Weather fine and observation good.	AJL
	18th		During the day Enemy shelled our front with a few rounds about every 5 minutes. At 10 pm Enemy was very quiet round of a suspicious nature. It was found that a party led our 1st Battn. required some avenging and arrangements were made for the troops to take over on the inside took place at 2 a.m. on the left Company rate Left Battalion. We spent a barrage and as a result the enemy were not up. The Brigade were complimented for work done by the Brigadier Brigade (144) who we were supporting. Communication were SOS delivered Red & white & alone by an adj. and there were repaired by this engineers mentioned fine. The action ended. I have 7 Brigade to which we replied. Slackers quiet.	AJL
	19th		Some shelling took place on our trenches.	AJL
	20th		Situation normal. All quiet.	AJL
	21st		10 officers + 30 N.C.O's from of the 31st Division attached.	AJL
	22nd		Attached officers & men of 31st Div. left at 9.30 a.m. All quiet on our front.	AJL
	23rd		Rain & mist, observation bad. Situation normal.	AJL
	24th		Gas alarm during night & harder part of morning. At shells fell in Hebuterne; only isolated fire reported.	AJL

Army Form C. 2118

WAR DIARY
or
INTELLIGENCE SUMMARY
(Erase heading not required.)

Instructions regarding War Diaries and Intelligence Summaries are contained in F. S. Regs., Part II. and the Staff Manual respectively. Title Pages will be prepared in manuscript.

Place	Date	Hour	Summary of Events and Information	Remarks and references to Appendices
COLINCAMPS	March 25th 1916		Situation quiet - Snow + rain. Machine fire; observation good. All quiet on our front.	AAL
	26th		Situation quiet; snow fell during night 25/26th.	AAL
	27th		Draft for new battery arrived at THIEVRES. 3 Officers + 136 N. COT + men.	AAL
	28th		Weather misty with rain; enemy quiet.	AAL
	29th		Situation normal. New battery formed at THIEVRES + roll call at 7.30pm, Capt Stone in command.	AAL
	30th		Situation normal. Enemy activity with rifle grenade + MINNENWERFERS on our trenches. This was effectually countered by our own trench mortars.	AAL
	31st		Weather fine, observation good. Enemy aeroplane stallion active. During afternoon from 2.30 to 4.30pm enemy fired about 150 150 m/m hours into S.W corner of COLINCAMPS, probably searching for the 9.2 hows who had been firing whilst enemy balloons + aeroplanes were up. Considerable damage was done to buildings in this portion of the village. 3rd Hows + 7 K.M.R batteries returned by x/169 Battery. One section of each. Gunnners lift in carriages + section of M/169 Battery 3/2 DIV respectfully. dialsights only being taken away by attacked	AAL

Crawford
LIEUT. COLONEL, R.F.A.
COMMANDING
240th (S.M.) Bde. R.F.A

SECRET

Original.
~~Duplicate~~

CONFIDENTIAL

War Diary

of

1/1st South Midland Brigade R.F.A.

From 1st April to 30th April 1916

Volume XXI

Crawford
LIEUT. COLONEL, R.F.A.
COMMANDING
240th (S.M.) BDE. R.F.A.

SECRET

Army Form C. 2118

WAR DIARY
or
INTELLIGENCE SUMMARY
(Erase heading not required.)

Instructions regarding War Diaries and Intelligence Summaries are contained in F. S. Regs., Part II. and the Staff Manual respectively. Title Pages will be prepared in manuscript.

Place	Date	Hour	Summary of Events and Information	Remarks and references to Appendices
COLINCAMPS April	1st	19.16	Weather fine. Enemy balloons active. Battery + m.g. fire very active with a/c patrols. This was silenced by our fire. Renewed all quiet. Remaining sections of 3rd Bde + independent batteries relieved this evening. The right half of our sector having been taken over by A + B batteries of the 169 Brigade. 3rd battery returns to COUENEUX for rest.	A.A.1.
	2nd		Situation normal. Enemy sent over a few rounds on different parts of our front during evening. The situation appears on both sides active.	A.A.1.
	3rd		Weather fine, mid/early morning thunder observation good. Except for about 15 minutes rifle + m.g. fire zone during afternoon generally, enemy normal.	J.A.1.
	4th		Weather fine but dull. Observations not good. Hostile artillery inactive.	A.A.1.
	5th		Weather fine. Situation normal. Intermittent shelling on both sides.	A.A.1.
COLINCAMPS – SAILLY	6th		This Brigade moved to SAILLY. The 169 Brigade of the 36 Division taking over. The Brigade front now extends from 3rd Avenue on the N. HEBUTERNE – SERRE road to LUKE COPSE to the by the 1st + 2nd batteries. The 3rd + D batteries are at rest. Mt. Hannaman and 60 men from D battery clothed this morning in new gun positions in orchards at HEBUTERNE approx. Grid ref number K.15.d. 6.8.	A.A.1.

WAR DIARY or INTELLIGENCE SUMMARY

Army Form C. 2118

(Erase heading not required.)

Instructions regarding War Diaries and Intelligence Summaries are contained in F. S. Regs., Part II. and the Staff Manual respectively. Title Pages will be prepared in manuscript.

Place	Date	Hour	Summary of Events and Information	Remarks and references to Appendices
SAILLY au BOIS	6th April 1916		Matters fairly situation normal during day. At 9.5 p.m. enemy opened a bombardment more or less on the trenches of 2g Th Div in front of MAILLY-MAILLET. At the commencement some shells also fell on our brigade front extending in report from our front to the R. of 2nd battery. There was slow barrage rifle & machine gun fire. This was apparently stopped on hearing from the infantry that the enemy bombardment extended further than the trenches at first. The enemy shelling lasted about an hour.	A.A.1.
	7th		Situation normal. About midday enemy guns fired on trenches into HEBUTERNE.	A.A.2.
	8th		Machine gun & intermittent shelling through day. At 6.15 p.m. enemy aeroplane dropped 2 bombs just west of trenches K.15.d. No damage done.	A.A.R.
	9th		Morning hazy. German artillery fire normal. We retaliated on several enemy trench mortars at Rqluet of our infantry. At 12.35 a.m. a hostile aeroplane dropped four bombs near K.32.c.1. Inbet - west of No 1 battery; no their situation normal.	A.A.3.

Army Form C. 2118

WAR DIARY
or
INTELLIGENCE SUMMARY
(Erase heading not required.)

Instructions regarding War Diaries and Intelligence Summaries are contained in F.S. Regs., Part II. and the Staff Manual respectively. Title Pages will be prepared in manuscript.

Place	Date	Hour	Summary of Events and Information	Remarks and references to Appendices
SAILLY April	10th	1916	Situation normal. During the night 10th/11th a new trench was dug joining points K10d.5.4 and K17c.0390. The digging party consisted of 100 men with covering party of 8 pros. Enemy artillery during operations inactive; only about 30 slight casualties received.	A.A.J.
	11th		Rain. Observation poor. Situation during day normal. Between the hours of 9 pm & 11 pm enemy Verey lights & new trench intermittently. Several flashes were taken from 207. At 2 new day 3rd battery relieved the 2nd battery taking over guns & numbers & 2.1.B. upon Indies. Weather previous to COIGNEUX forest.	A.A.J.
	12th 13th		Heavy rain all day. Observation poor. Hostile fire nil. All quiet. Rain but cleared by evening when observation became good. Intermittent artillery fire on both sides. At 9.45 pm 3 Red rockets were sent up from N.9.d.individual. No hostile action followed. At 11 pm again at 3.30 pm enemy trench fire in Northern trench east of HÉBUTERNE. In each case hostile fire only lasted about 5 minutes.	A.A.J. A.A.J.
	14th		Situation quiet. Observation good & enemy movements seen behind the lines. At 6.45 am a monoplane heard and flying S.W. It was prominent design marked with British marks. Our anti-aircraft fire fired 3 rounds at it.	A.A.J.

WAR DIARY
or
INTELLIGENCE SUMMARY

Army Form C. 2118

Place	Date	Hour	Summary of Events and Information	Remarks and references to Appendices
SAILLY April	22nd 1916		Heavy rain. Enemy artillery inactive. Nothing to report.	A.A.1.
	23rd		Lt Col. A.M. BALFOUR left this morning for England. Weather fine. Enemy shelled our trenches during the afternoon. Enemy active with observation balloons. We disposed a enemy party during the afternoon. 5 companies of infantry observed marching from PUISIEUX to BUCQUOY. Each company about 150 strong. First shot fired at 12.15pm by 3rd Battery.	A.A.2.
	24th		Enemy artillery quiet during day. At about 11.30pm enemy bombarded our trench east of HEBUTERNE, mostly with MINENWERFERS. It lasted about 10 minutes.	A.A.3.
	25th		Situation normal, nothing to report.	A.B.1.
	26th		Intermittent artillery on both sides. 5.15am to 6.45am hostile battery fired at T15c line shelled. No casualties. About 110 rounds. Further	A.A.2.
	27th		Between 7am + 8am enemy shelled 3rd Battery positions with 15 cm hows. About 156 rounds. Two direct hits on No.3 Gun Emplacement were registered. No other casualties of any kind was hit. Consequently little damage was done. The hostile battery was located at Q20 a 53 (S). There was considerable activity from this battery throughout the day. Otherwise situation normal.	A.B.3.
	29th		At about 4am hostile aeroplane dropped 2 bombs in SAILLY. It was not engaged by our anti-aircraft guns. From 9am to 11am enemy battery at ? shelled "C"	A.A.1.

WAR DIARY
or
INTELLIGENCE SUMMARY.

(Erase heading not required.)

Army Form C. 2118.

Hour, Date, Place 1916.	Summary of Events and Information	Remarks and references to Appendices
SAILLY April 28th	Position with 211-15cm. shells. Observation good throughout day, a number of working parties observed and those within range were dispersed by our fire. A train was observed proceeding from BUCQUOY to PUISIEUX laden with timber.	J.A.
" 29th.	Situation normal. No enemy movements seen. One working party dispersed by our fire. Anti-aircraft gun at 4.20d very active. Flashes observed & battery engaged by us. 11pm to 12:30am Heavy bombardment south of our front. 2nd Battery went into "C" position tonight - taking over the line from K.17d.1.9 to K.11c.8.5.	N.M.
" 30th.	Several working parties were dispersed by our fire during the day - Hostile fire normal, night quiet.	J.A.

Lieut. Colonel, R.F.A.
Commanding
240th (S.M.) Bde. R.F.A.

Army Form C. 2118

WAR DIARY
or
INTELLIGENCE SUMMARY
(Erase heading not required.)

Instructions regarding War Diaries and Intelligence Summaries are contained in F.S. Regs., Part II. and the Staff Manual respectively. Title Pages will be prepared in manuscript.

Place	Date	Hour	Summary of Events and Information	Remarks and references to Appendices
SAILLY. April	15th 1916		Situation normal. Between 9.45 & 10.4pm two enemy shells nr new trench with about 100 T/Min too MINNENWERFERS.	A.A.S.
	16th		Observation good. Several working parties and a machine gun effectively engaged by our artillery during that hour. Enemy active with balloons/artillery inactive. 2/Lt. E.M. J. Polen joins this brigade from 3rd Line. (Appointment to/Sept. 3. 1. 16)	A.S.S.
	17th		Situation normal. Raining nearly all day. Enemy again bombarded our new trench east of Fonquevillers between 10.30 & 11 pm. 10 party of enemy men observed slipping in a long new trench east of PUISIEUX. It was reported to many Brigades but they were never found (the one of range)	A.S.S.
	18th		Heavy rain all day. During afternoon enemy working party dispersed by our fire. The new trench east of Fpt Station again subjected to intermittent bombardment from about 9 pm till midnight, phosphorus situation quiet.	A.A.L
	19th		Rain; situation normal. We again dispersed enemy working parties during the day.	A A L
	20th		Rain; situation normal. Between 3 pm & 4 pm about 120 15 cms shells fell on & around B position. The Brigade front shortened; now extends from K 9.d.1.5½ to K 23.d.8.4.	A.S.S.
	21st		Rain; situation quiet. 17 m/min battery locations at L 14.a.7.2 & 7 transferred to CRA.	A.A.S.

Original SECRET

CONFIDENTIAL

Vol 13 14 15

War Diary

of

240th (S. Mid) Brigade R.F.A.

From May 1st to May 31st 1916

late 1/1 S.M Bde

Volume XXII

[signature]

LIEUT. COLONEL, R.F.A.
COMMANDING
240th (S.M.) BDE. R.F.A.

Army Form C. 2118.

WAR DIARY
or
INTELLIGENCE SUMMARY.
(Erase heading not required.)

Hour, Date, Place	Summary of Events and Information	Remarks and references to Appendices
SAILLY May 1st.	Between 9:30 a.m. to 10:30 a.m. enemy battery at L20a1.25 shelled SAILLY. J19a probably in search of the 60 pdr. battery. Intermittent artillery fire on both sides. Several working parties were dispersed during the day. 4 p.m. Germans seen marching from PUISIEUX to BUCQUOY about 100 strong and wearing dark uniforms.	A.A.L.
" 2nd.	Situation normal. Usual artillery activity on both sides. 2.10 p.m. Train (10 trucks) observed travelling between PUISIEUX - BUCQUOY.	A.A.L.
" 3rd.	There was considerable amount of work going on behind the German lines today. All parties within range were dispersed. Nothing unusual to report.	A.A.L.
" 4th.	Situation normal. The Germans are digging a new trench in L7a.	A.A.L.

WAR DIARY or INTELLIGENCE SUMMARY

Army Form C. 2118

Place	Date	Hour	Summary of Events and Information	Remarks and references to Appendices
SAILLY	May 5th	1916	Brigade office moved to No. 97 Redoubt SAILLY. 2/Lt. J.G. Barrett joined this Brigade from the 3rd Divn. Situation normal. Several enemy working parties were dispersed by our fire during the day. The Germans were wearing a searchlight between 9.30 p.m. & 10 p.m. in neighbourhood opposite FUX.	A.A.I.
	6th		Hostile artillery less active than usual. During night 17ph another 60 yds of trench was dug in L7a.7.1	A.A.I.
	7th		Hostile artillery again quiet during day. Our fire stopped work at K.7.d. a.6.4. When there appeared to be despatch differs. Several direct hits were obtained which enfilade the front of enemy were certain. Post card. From Germans were seen in front of PUISIEUX wearing dark blue uniforms. Between 11.30 p.m. & 12-30 a.m. enemy bombarded our trenches & roads at COLINCAMPS.	A.A.I.
	8th		Situation quiet. Right section of 2nd Battery moved into new position. Indications at K.3.rd.3.4. Right section of 2nd Howr Battery came into position K.3rd.3.2. under temporary command of Capt. Phillips. Considerable amount of troops & transports in BUCQUOY & ACHIET during afternoon.	A.A.I.
	9th		Rain. Enemy attempts artillery inactive. New monied howr. up at L.5.d.3.4. Our Brigade Craft Rew hour 3rd Brigade into returned to their waggon lines to rest.	A.A.I.

Army Form C. 2118

WAR DIARY
or
INTELLIGENCE SUMMARY
(Erase heading not required.)

Instructions regarding War Diaries and Intelligence Summaries are contained in F.S. Regs., Part II. and the Staff Manual respectively. Title Pages will be prepared in manuscript.

Place	Date	Hour	Summary of Events and Information	Remarks and references to Appendices
SAILLY	May 9th	10.16	LIEUT. COL. LORD WYNFORD took over command of the brigade today.	A.A.A.
	10th		Enemy shelled HEBUTERNE with 15 cm. how. shells this morning between 7 & 8.15 am; otherwise no artillery activity on either side was noted. Trains were observed going to from BUCQUOY & ACHIET LE PETIT during the afternoon. There was considerable traffic on road between BUCQUOY and ACHIET LE PETIT which increased towards dusk.	A.A.
	11th		Situation normal. Nothing to report.	A.A.
	12th		HEBUTERNE was shelled this morning with about 20 15 cm. how. & 77 m/m shrapnel. Enemy artillery was active throughout the day. Our front line Trench K.5 g.d. to K.5 g.k. appeared to be being registered. Between 3 & 3.15 pm.	A.A.
	13th		HEBUTERNE was again shelled this morning. About 200 15 cm how. shells fell into & East of the K.10.a. Between 8.15 g am. & 1.10 am how. shells were fired into our trenches K.5.b. & K.10.d. during considerable damage. A range from 245 pm. to 9.45 pm. hostile 15 cm. how. shelling at about 9.70 fired about 30 rounds into K.5.c. & K. roads. No damage was done. Throughout the day observation was poor. Night quiet.	A.A.

WAR DIARY
or
INTELLIGENCE SUMMARY
(Erase heading not required.)

Army Form C. 2118

Place	Date	Hour	Summary of Events and Information	Remarks and references to Appendices
SAILLY	May 14th 1916		Rain, observation poor. We disposed several enemy working parties during the day. Enemy artillery quiet & observant normal.	Q.Q.d.
	15th 1916		Weather fine. Enemy artillery inactive; all quiet	A.A.d.
	16th 1916		During the night 15/16 from 12.15 a.m. till 2.20 a.m. a hostile raid was made on our trenches opposite the POINT K23.b.1.8. The Germans came down the CHASSEURS HEDGE. Our trenches were heavily shelled, with 5.9 cm howrs; our batteries were all active. From 8–10 A.M. our 2nd Battery in K20 d.1.6. had 200 5.9 cm hours all about the position but no casualties occurred. For the remainder of the day the situation was normal.	A.A.d.
	17th 1916		Fine. Observation good. Very little activity. From midnight 17/18 the Brigade ceased to be called the 1st SOUTH MIDLAND BRIGADE R.F.A.. It was given the title of 240th (S.M.) BRIGADE R.F.A. & the batteries instead of being called 1st 2nd & 3rd S.M. were called A, B, & D batteries. The 4th Howitzer Battery became part of (4th S.M. Brigade)	A.A.d.

D. Ashley

WAR DIARY
or
INTELLIGENCE SUMMARY
(Erase heading not required.)

Army Form C. 2118

Place	Date	Hour	Summary of Events and Information	Remarks and references to Appendices
SAILLY	17		The Brigade was called D battery. The following officers came with D battery. MAJOR C. FOWLER. LIEUTS. H d'R. VAILLANCEY, W. WYLEY, F. B. BRODRIBB. 2nd LIEUTS. J. P. NICKALLS (acting Adjutant), A. T. LOWE (supernumerary).	A.A.L.
	18.		Hostile artillery inactive. Fine, observation good. At 3p.m.	A.A.L.
			The 9.2 fired on the POINT K23 b.1.8. 9 of our batteries fired in conjunction with them for an hour. In the course of the day several working parties were dispersed.	
	19.		Fine, observation very poor owing to a ground haze. Situation quite normal.	A.A.L.
	20.		Fine, observation good. In the afternoon morning 9-9.55 the HEBUTERNE-SAILLY road was shelled with 16.7mm. The enemy's train transport was active in the region of PUISIEUX. Infantry were seen from 4.30p.m. till dusk in many lodges moving in ones from a platoon to a company with transport moving N (wards) BUCQUOY presumably from ACHIET.	A.A.L.

Army Form C. 2118

WAR DIARY
or
INTELLIGENCE SUMMARY
(Erase heading not required.)

Instructions regarding War Diaries and Intelligence Summaries are contained in F.S. Regs., Part II. and the Staff Manual respectively. Title Pages will be prepared in manuscript.

Place	Date	Hour	Summary of Events and Information	Remarks and references to Appendices
SAILLY				
May	21.		Fine. Very little firing was done by our batteries. About 100	A.A.L.
			15 cm (How) shells fell in the QUARRIES, K 21 b 5,8. at 8 A.M.	A.A.L.
	22.		THE QUARRIES were again shelled: 35 rounds (15 cm).	A.A.L.
	23.		Hostile artillery more active than usual. 14 15 cm rounds fell in	
			COLINCAMPS about 3 p.m.; 1 round falling in the yard of A battery	
			billet. Four infantry officers were attached to the Brigade,	
			(one to each battery) for the purpose of instruction for 4 days.	A.A.L.
	24.		Very misty, observation very poor. Very little activity.	
	25.		Observation again poor. The enemy's artillery was active between 10.30 & 11 a.m.	A.A.L.
			At the request of the infantry a concentrated retaliation was successfully carried out—	
			by A, B, & D batteries.	
	26.		Situation quite normal. A few working parties were dispersed.	A.A.L.
	27.		Hostile aeroplanes shows more enterprise than usual; planes were seen over PUISIEUX,	
			SERRE, COLINCAMPS & SAILLY. SAILLY was shelled in the afternoon	
			by 5.9 cm Howitzers & 77 mm gun. A few casualties occurred in the village. The Cook	
			on the Brigade Headquarters staff was hit by a small piece of shrapnel. Very slight wound.	A.A.L.

WAR DIARY
or
INTELLIGENCE SUMMARY

Army Form C. 2118

(Erase heading not required.)

Place	Date	Hour	Summary of Events and Information	Remarks and references to Appendices
SAILLY May.	28.		Our artillery inactive: a few working parties were dispersed. A hostile battery in front of PUISIEUX heavily shelled a 60 pdr. battery in the SOUTH side of SAILLY slightly damaging 2 guns. Four Infantry officers were attached to the Brigade (one to each battery) for instruction.	A.Ad.
	29.		Situation normal. A hostile plane flew over our trenches (recently dug) in K.10.d. & K.16.a.	A.Ad.
	30.		Rain. Observation very difficult. Activity during the day normal. Between 12 & 1 am, the enemy were active with canister bombs on our trenches opposite the POINT & the HOOK, K.23.a.&.b. An organised bombardment by A & C batteries has the desired effect.	A.Ad.
	31.		Owing to the enemy's activity in the POINT & the HOOK K23.a.d A, C & D batteries combined with the 9.2's in bombarding these two points & the communication trenches running up from them, with some success.	A.Ad.

LIEUT. COLONEL
COMMANDING
40th (S.M.) BDE. R.F.A.

CONFIDENTIAL

WAR DIARY

of

240ᵀᴴ (S.M.) BRIGADE R.F.A.

for

JUNE 1916.

Crawford

Lieut. Colonel, R.F.A.
Commanding
240th (S.M.) Bde. R.F.A.

WAR DIARY or INTELLIGENCE SUMMARY

Army Form C. 2118

Place	Date	Hour	Summary of Events and Information	Remarks and references to Appendices
SAILLY	June 1st		Very little activity on our part. In retaliation apparently for an organised bombardment the enemy took K25 b.d. & both 15 cm How battery in B17Z wood K.1.b. Shelled C battery heavily this morning. No casualties occurred though two direct hits were made on No.2 gunpit; the concrete proved an excellent shelter. A great deal of traffic wagons & lorries was observed on the BUCQUOY – PUISIEUX road.	AAA.
	2nd		Hostile batteries active. A 15 cm battery from Rossignol wood K1.b. shelled S.F. position of H.F. Battery. Staining a direct hit on the officers dugout. Of C Battery which did not penetrate. This battery in conjunction with a 105 cm battery shelled our new trenches in K16.b, but did little damage. The above 15 cm How battery again shelled our trenches in K16.b, in the morning for about an hour & a half, sending one round over every 3 minutes. With the exception of a little registering our batteries were inactive.	AAA.
	3rd		'A' battery was lent to the 31st Division for the night of 3/4 who were carrying out a raiding operation on the enemy trenches in K28 d & K29 a. The raid was fairly successful though a few casualties occurred in the raiding party.	AAA.
	4th		On the night 4/5 the Brigade was relieved by 243 (S.M.) Brigade & came out into rest to the wagon lines at COLINCAMPS. The first time the Brigade as a whole has been in rest since July 19/15 [illegible]	AAA.
	5th			

WAR DIARY
or
INTELLIGENCE SUMMARY

Army Form C. 2118

Place	Date	Hour	Summary of Events and Information	Remarks and references to Appendices
COIGNEUX	June 6th	-	Wet. Batteries were at disposal of Battery Commanders. Guns of A and B batteries were inspected by I.O.M. VIII Corps. One gun was found to be needing adjustment.	A.A.d.
	7th	-	Wet. Battery Commanders instructed their Battery Staffs. Guns of C Battery were inspected by I.O.M.	A.A.d.
	8th	-	Morning fine - later wet. The Brigade and Battery commanders with their Staffs reconnoitred line to be held and positions to be occupied by our batteries in case of retreat.	A.A.d.
	9th	-	Last night 8th-9th D/240 Battery was relieved in action by D/241 Battery and joined the Brigade at COIGNEUX. A and B Batteries practiced their Battery Staffs. C Battery had Drill Order. C.O. held a conference of all the officers of the Brigade.	A.M.
	10th	-	More rain. The Brigade paraded in full marching order and was inspected by C.O., afterwards going for a route march.	A.A.d.
	11th	-	Fine. Battery Horse Lines were inspected by C.O. Brigade Church Parade was held in the afternoon and was attended by C.R.A. Memorial Service for Field Marshall Lord Kitchener.	A.A.d.

WAR DIARY or INTELLIGENCE SUMMARY

Army Form C. 2118

(Erase heading not required.)

Instructions regarding War Diaries and Intelligence Summaries are contained in F. S. Regs., Part II. and the Staff Manual respectively. Title Pages will be prepared in manuscript.

Place	Date	Hour	Summary of Events and Information	Remarks and references to Appendices
	June 12th	-	Showery. Battery Commanders practised their Battery Staffs.	WR 7th
	13	-	Showery. Orders were received to stop training and work to be pushed on on various Battery positions in course of construction. C/110 Battery relieved A/143 Battery in action.	WR 7th
	14		Morning Showery. Afternoon fine. Work on gun positions continued.	WR 7th
	15		Fine. A.C.D Batteries went back into action in the positions they have just made.	WR 7th
	16		Fine. Work of finishing Battery positions was carried on.	WR 7th
	17		Work on gun positions was continued. Brigade headquarters moved from Coigneux to SAILLY.	WR 7th
SAILLY	18 19 20 21 22 23		Work was continued on Battery positions. During this period ammunition to the amount of 1,000 rounds per gun for 18 Pdrs and 800 for 4.5 howitzers was dumped at gun positions. On 19th Lieut WR D Wylly took over duties of Adjt from Capt. WR Benson.	WR 7th W.
	24		Bombardment began 5 am. A and B Batteries carried out wire cutting operations	

Army Form C. 2118

WAR DIARY
or
INTELLIGENCE SUMMARY
(Erase heading not required.)

Place	Date	Hour	Summary of Events and Information	Remarks and references to Appendices
SAILLY	June 24 (cont)		on German 3rd and 2nd line, respectively, 1000 yards north of SERRE. C Battery bombarded suspected O.P's, and M.G. emplacements in same area. D Battery bombarded Trench Junctions and Communication Trenches in the same area. 18 Pdrs fired 125 rounds per gun and 4.5 howitzers 120 rounds per gun. Bombardment was carried on during the night. A Battery had one man killed and one man wounded. B Battery two men and C Battery one man wounded.	1 SR 1 h
	25		Bombardment was continued; the batteries carrying out the same duties as the previous day. During the night 25/6 there was a discharge of gas from our trenches.	1 SR 1 h
	26		Bombardment continued. During the morning the discharge of gas was successfully repeated. From 9 am to 10.30 am C and D Batteries co-operated with the VIII Corps Heavy Artillery Groups in a concentrated bombardment of enemy first and second line.	1 SR 1 h
	27		The bombardment was again continued. C + D Batteries again combined with the Heavy Artillery and bombarded the enemy's 3rd line trenches from 5.30 am to 6.30 am and much damage was done to SERRE by heavy howitzers. In the afternoon A Battery completed wire cutting on their own front, proceeded to cut the front line wire on the N. of 31st Div Front.	1 SR 1 h
	28		At 5 am there was another special bombardment by the Heavy Artillery, but owing to heavy mist observation was practically impossible. The mist cleared about 11.30 a.m. when wire cutting was continued	Q 1 h

Army Form C. 2118

WAR DIARY
or
INTELLIGENCE SUMMARY
(Erase heading not required.)

Instructions regarding War Diaries and Intelligence Summaries are contained in F. S. Regs., Part II. and the Staff Manual respectively. Title Pages will be prepared in manuscript.

Place	Date	Hour	Summary of Events and Information	Remarks and references to Appendices
SAILLY.	June 29th		The day of Assault having been postponed for 48 hours, the bombardment was continued.	WRTW
	June 30th		The Preliminary Bombardment was concluded.	WRTW

LIEUT: COLONEL, R.F.A.
COMMANDING
240th (S.M.) BDE. R.F.A.

WAR DIARY

Headquarters,

240th BRIGADE, R.F.A.

(48th Division)

J U L Y

1 9 1 6

CONFIDENTIAL

Vol 17

VOLUME 16.

WAR DIARY

OF

240TH (S.M.) BRIGADE R.F.A.

FOR PERIOD

1ST JULY to 31ST JULY 1916.

[signature]
LIEUT. COLONEL. R.F.A.
COMMANDING
240th (S.M.) BDE. R.F.A.

WAR DIARY or INTELLIGENCE SUMMARY

Army Form C. 2118

Place	Date	Hour	Summary of Events and Information	Remarks and references to Appendices
SAILLY	July 1st	1.	Day of Assault. Fine. At 6.30 a.m. the final intense bombardment started. At 7.30 a.m. the 31st Div. on the right of the 48th assaulted the trenches infront of SERRE. Owing to a thick mist and smoke it was impossible to observe the progress of the attack, but later in the day it was reported that the attack had not succeeded, and by the night of 1/2nd the survivors of the battalions taking part in the attack had returned to their own trenches. During the attack – until 12 noon – the 48th Div. Artillery covered its left flank, 18-Pdrs firing about 2,000 rounds per battery and 4.5" Howitzers about 1,500 rounds per Battery. During the days of bombardment and the day of assault the Brigade casualties were :- 1 Officer and 9 Ranks killed – 9 Ranks wounded.	WRFW
		2.	Comparatively quiet on VIII Corps front, except for two bombardments which took place in the afternoon and lasted about ½ hour each.	WRFW
		3.	Nothing to report – weather fine.	WRFW
		4.	Very heavy rain storms. During the nights 3/4 and 4/5 A and B batteries fired on tracks leading to the trenches from PUISIEUX. D battery fired on road junctions between SERRE and PUISIEUX.	WRFW
		5.	A battery recorded wire cutting on 31st Divisional front which has now been taken over by 144th Brigade. During the night 5/6 B, C & D batteries fired bursts of fire on the Cross roads behind the German lines.	WRFW

Army Form C. 2118

WAR DIARY or INTELLIGENCE SUMMARY
(Erase heading not required.)

Place	Date	Hour	Summary of Events and Information	Remarks and references to Appendices
SAILLY.	6th July.		Fine and comparatively quiet day. C Battery was shelled during the afternoon. Same activity displayed by the brigade as during previous night.	WR4W
	7		O.C. Brigade held Battery commanders conference at C Battery, to discuss programme of firing for next few days. Very heavy thunderstorms.	WR4W
	8 "		The wire cutting which was carried on previous day was cancelled and batteries confined themselves to firing on any movement seen, and bombarding places in enemy's trenches where work was done previous night.	WR4W
	9th		Line. Batteries carried out same programme as on 8th.	WR4W
	10th		Line. Batteries carried out same programme as on 8th and 9th.	WR4W
	11th		Line Lt-Colonel A.R.B. Cowart, commanding 242 Brigade having taken over command of "A" Group, Divisional Artillery, consisting of 240th and 242nd Brigades, the Brigade H.Q. went into Camp at COIGNEUX.	WR4W WR4W
COIGNEUX.	12th		Line. A/240 Battery moved from wire cutting position on southern edge of HEBUTERNE to position in the orchards S.E. of SAILLY.	WR4W
	13th		Showery. At 11.20 p.m. the Brigade bombarded enemy's trenches north of POINT in conjunction with 242nd Brigade covering a raid which was carried out by 144th Infantry Bde.	WR4W
	14th		3.15am to 3.30 am Brigade carried out intense bombardment of enemy 1st and 2nd line trenches N and S of THE POINT. 11.22 pm Large working party round POINT was fired at and dispersed by C Battery.	WR4W

Army Form C. 2118

WAR DIARY
or
INTELLIGENCE SUMMARY
(Erase heading not required.)

Instructions regarding War Diaries and Intelligence Summaries are contained in F.S. Regs., Part II. and the Staff Manual respectively. Title Pages will be prepared in manuscript.

Place	Date	Hour	Summary of Events and Information	Remarks and references to Appendices
COIGNEUX	15th July		Line. The 48th Divisional moved south and the 48th Divisional Artillery came under the command of 38th Division who relieved us & &c.	LRTN
	16th July		Line. Nothing to report.	LRTN
	17th "		Showery. Nothing to report.	LRTN
	18th "		Wet. Orders were received for 48th Divisional Artillery to relieve 12th Divisional Artillery in action near AVELUY.	LRTN
	19th "		Line. C.O. and Battery Commanders proceeded to ALBERT by motor bus to inspect the battery positions that will be taken over in the course of a few days by the Brigade.	LRTN
	20th "		Line. 120 L. Brigade, 38th Division, relieved batteries in action and latter proceeded to Wagon Line. COIGNEUX and stayed for night 20/21.	LRTN
AVELUY	21st "		Gun attachments travelled to AVELUY by motor bus to take over guns of 12th Division Artillery in action near this village. The remainder of Brigade marched to Wagon Line, near BOUZINCOURT. Brigade H.Q. were established in AVELUY WOOD, in company with 243rd Bde H.Q. which took over command Northern Group Divisional Artillery, consisting of 243rd Brigade and C/240 Bty and L B/240 Bty as a six gun battery under O/C C/240 Battery and D/240 Battery. A/240 Battery and other half	LRTN

WAR DIARY
or
INTELLIGENCE SUMMARY

Army Form C. 2118

Place	Date	Hour	Summary of Events and Information	Remarks and references to Appendices
AVELUY	21/7/16		B/240 Battery came under command of Lt-Colonel. A.R.B. COSSART. commanding Southern Group Divisional Artillery.	LRM
"	22/7/16		Line. Left Group covered front running roughly E and W; 1000 yards north of OVILLERS and retiring 1500 yards up old German front line trenches. During the night flare were kept up on the German trenches and communication trenches. OPs were established just to the north of OVILLERS.	LRM
"	23/7/16		Line. Comparatively quiet day. At 8.30 p.m. (night of 23/24) a four hour bombardment was started. At 12.30 am the 144th and 145 Infantry Brigades in conjunction with the ANZACS on their right attacked enemy trenches running from North POZIERES for 2,000 yards to north of OVILLERS. The 145th Infantry Brigade succeeded in obtaining their objective and the ANZACS occupied positions of POZIERES	LRM
"	24/7/16		Line. During the day bursts of fire were kept up in support of the Infantry who were consolidating their gains. During the early part of the afternoon the enemy attempted a counter attack on the North of POZIERES. This was stopped by our Artillery fire.	LRM
"	25/7/16		Dull but fine. During the course of the day the Bridge-heads on the East of the ANCRE and our battery positions near them were shelled with lachrymatory shells.	LRM

WAR DIARY or INTELLIGENCE SUMMARY

Army Form C. 2118

Place	Date	Hour	Summary of Events and Information	Remarks and references to Appendices
AVELUY	26/7/16		Fine. Comparatively quiet day except for heavy shelling of POZIERES. During the afternoon the half of B Battery which had been attached to A/240 Battery took up advanced position in MASH VALLEY between OVILLERS and LA BOISSELLE. During nights 26/27 bursts of fire were kept up on enemy communication trenches and MOUQUET FARM.	MR/W
	27/7/16		Fine. The half B Battery joined the half in MASH VALLEY.	WR/W
	28/7/16		Fine. The half B Battery attached to A/240 Battery was relieved in action by 65th Brigade, 12th Div. and proceeded to its wagon lines near BOUZINCOURT where it bivouaced for the night.	WR/W
AMPLIER	29/7/16		Fine. The Brigade marched to AMPLIER via PUTHIE and SARTON.	WR/W
	30/7/16		Fine. The Brigade continued its march to ST. OUEN via DOULLENS and DOMART, where it went into rest.	WR/W
	31/7/16		Fine.	WR/W

Lieut. Colonel, R.F.A.
Commanding
240th (S.M.) Bde. R.F.A.

48th Divisional Artillery

240th (South Midland) BRIGADE

ROYAL FIELD ARTILLERY

AUGUST 1 9 1 6 ::::::

CONFIDENTIAL   ORIGINAL

Vol 8   VOLUME 7.

WAR DIARY

OF

240TH (S.M.) BRIGADE, R.F.A.

for period

1ST AUG. to 31ST AUG 1916.

[signature]
LIEUT. COLONEL, R.F.A.
COMMANDING
240th (S.M.) Bde., R.F.A.

Army Form C. 2118

WAR DIARY
or
INTELLIGENCE SUMMARY
(Erase heading not required.)

Place	Date	Hour	Summary of Events and Information	Remarks and references to Appendices
ST. OUEN	1st Aug to 8th Aug		The Brigade was at rest.	WRTW
	9th/8/16		The Brigade marched to Amplier via – CANDAS and BEAUVAL.	WRTW
AMPLIER	10/8/16		Fine but dull.	
	11/8/16		Fine. The Brigade rested. B.C.'s travelled by motor bus to positions to be taken over near OVILLERS.	WRTW
	12/8/16		Fine. The Brigade continued it's march to wagon lines previously occupied near BOUZINCOURT, where it bivouaced for the night.	WRTW
BOUZINCOURT	13/8/16		Fine. Gun detachments marched to positions near OVILLERS and took over guns of 12th Div. Arty. in action. A/240 Battery and ½ B/240 Battery came under command of Lt-Col. A.R.B. COSSART commanding RIGHT GROUP DIVISIONAL ARTILLERY. C/240 Battery, ½ B/240 Battery and D/240 Battery came under command of Lt-Col WEST commanding LEFT GROUP DIVISIONAL ARTILLERY. The Brigade H.Q. remained at Wagon Lines.	WRTW
	14/8/16		Showery night 13/14 Enemy gained footing in SKYLINE TRENCH	WRTW
	15/9/16		night 14/15 Enemy ejected from SKYLINE TRENCH.	WRTW

WAR DIARY
or
INTELLIGENCE SUMMARY

Army Form C. 2118

Place	Date	Hour	Summary of Events and Information	Remarks and references to Appendices
BOUZIN-COURT	16/8/16		Guns of C/240 Battery and half B/240 Battery were lent to 25th Divisional Artillery. Personnel of batteries remained in position building new emplacements.	WR7W
	17/8/16		D/240 Battery fired 500 rounds THERMITE shell for experimental purpose.	WR7W
	18/8/16		Batteries supported attack by 143 Bde on trench N.E of Authille wood. This was successful.	WR7W
	19/8/16 20/8/16		Nothing to report. The Corps Commander personally commended O.C. Brigade for the fine work done by batteries on the occasion of the successful attack on 18th.	WR7W
	21/8/16		Infantry attacked trenches E of Leipzig Salient, supported by Divl. Arty.	WR7W
	22/8/16		C Battery received 4 guns.	WR7W
	23/8/16		Enemy artillery very active, particularly near CRUCIFIX CORNER where three bomb stores were blown up. 1003 Sergt PRICE W.V. was killed. Also Lieut E.L. GEDYE, the latter was in attempt to extinguish a fire in a bomb store.	WR7W
	24/8/16		Artillery carried out bombardment to assist 25th Div Infantry to attack HINDENBERG TRENCH. Its bofo Commander awarded	WR7W

WAR DIARY or INTELLIGENCE SUMMARY

Army Form C. 2118

Place	Date	Hour	Summary of Events and Information	Remarks and references to Appendices
BOUZINCOURT			Sergt. Makers J.	
	25/8/16		Military medal to k369 Bomb'r BOLLER.R.W. and 364 Br KING W. D/240 Battery. Enemy attacked HINDENBURG TRENCH but was repulsed by artillery fire. 26.9.M. 9. HAYES transferred from D/241 to D/240.	WRTW WRTW
	26/8/16		2/Lt. Gunyon and 2/Lt. BAINES joined Brigade from BASE. 48/9 wounded. Artillery had orders to take up positions under command of 49th Div. Arty. Lt.Col. THE LORD WINFORD to take command of HOWITZER GROUP, consisting of the following batteries D/240, D/241, D/242, D/246.	WRTW
	27/8/16		Battery Commanders reconnoitred new positions and O.P. Gunner MIDDLETON A No 546, D/240 was killed by premature. 3 Gr/ranks were wounded.	WRTW
AVELUY WOOD	28/8/16		Batteries took up new positions. The four batteries of How. Group occupied positions on western edge of AVELUY WOOD with Group H.Q. at the S.W. corner of the wood.	WRTW
	29/8/16		Batteries registered on enemy trenches N of THIEPVAL	WRTW
	30/8/16		Very Wet. Gale blowing. Under weather conditions registration was impossible. B.C. conference in the evening when 49th Div Arty Operation Orders were issued.	WRTW
	31/8/16		Registration of Communication Trenches between ST PIERRE DIVION and continued	WRTW

LIEUT. COLONEL, R.F.A.
COMMANDING

48th. DIVISIONAL ARTILLERY

240th. BRIGADE R. F. A.

SEPTEMBER 1 9 1 6.

48th. DIVISIONAL ARTILLERY

CONFIDENTIAL   ORIGINAL

Vol 19

VOLUME 18

WAR DIARY

of

240ᵀᴴ (SM) BRIGADE RFA

for period

1ˢᵀ SEPT. to 30ᵀᴴ SEPT 1916.

G.P. Brooke Taylor
Lieut
a/Adjutant
for Major
LIEUT. COLONEL, R.F.A.
COMMANDING
240th (S.M.) BDE. R.F.A.

WAR DIARY
or
INTELLIGENCE SUMMARY

Army Form C. 2118

240th Brigade, R.F.A.
48th (S.M.) Division

Place	Date	Hour	Summary of Events and Information	Remarks and references to Appendices
MESNIL	1/9/16		Quiet. Operations on THIEPVAL front postponed.	9, P & 9.
MESNIL	2/9/16		Wire cutting in Q.24.b.	9, P & 9.
MESNIL	3/9/16		Batteries checked their final registration for their next day's objective. 49th Division assaulted the German line between R.19.c.8.4. & the river ANCRE. Barrage opened at 5.10 A.M. & assault was made at 5.13 A.M. The infantry gained their objective on the South side of the river but were unable to hold it owing to the failure of the assault North of the river — which exposed them to machine-gun fire.	9, P & 9.
MESNIL	4/9/16		The Batteries were shelled during the day & 240 suffering casualties — 2 other ranks wounded. Fire kept up during the day on the Barrage lines of the day before. 'C' Battery was heavily shelled one gun being knocked out of action — casualties. 2/Lieut C.A. Jayatton & 7 other ranks wounded.	Q.P.B.9.
MESNIL	5/9/16		Firing normal. 'D' Battery experimented with gas shells. 'C' Battery was shelled, one gun being put out of action. Enemy shelled the MESNIL valley every night with tear shells.	Q.P.B.9.
BOUZINCOURT	6/9/16		Personnel of battery — with the exception of a small guard — was withdrawn to the wagon lines.	Q.P.B.9.
BOUZINCOURT	7/9/16		Personnel remained at the wagon lines, parties being sent up to keep working at the battery positions.	Q.P.B.9.
BOUZINCOURT	8/9/16			
BOUZINCOURT	9/9/16		Nothing to report.	
BOUZINCOURT	10/9/16			
BOUZINCOURT	11/9/16			Q.P.B.9.
BOUZINCOURT	12/9/16		Corporal Rice of 'C' Battery awarded the Military Medal. Batteries returned into action. 'C' Battery to the same position.	
BOUZINCOURT	13/9/16		at Q.34.b.3.8. 'B' Battery split up, 1 section joined 'C' Battery to the same position. 'A' Battery to new position. Gun of line 'B' Battery awarded the Military Medal. 'C' Battery & the other A/242 combined group of 240 & 243 Brigades assisted 11th Division in the attack upon the wonderwork in R.31.c.30.15. The attack being entirely successful.	Q.P.B.9.

Army Form C. 2118

240th Brigade R.F.A.
48th [S.M.] Division

WAR DIARY
or
INTELLIGENCE SUMMARY
(Erase heading not required.)

Place	Date	Hour	Summary of Events and Information	Remarks and references to Appendices
BOUZINCOURT	15/9/16		All batteries came out of action early in the morning & returned to the wagon lines. Extensive operations were reported from the districts of COURCELETTE & Brigade held itself in readiness to move at two hours notice. Orders were received to move at 2.20 a.m. The Brigade was commanded by Major Porter (O/C "D" Battery) owing to the indisposition of Lt. Col. the Lord Wynford. The Brigade marched via BOUZINCOURT - ALBERT to an open position in X.9.b.8.2. wagon lines being established at W.24.a.2.8. Fire was opened at 6.20 p.m. in the road R.29.a.5.9 to R.29.a.8.7. in support of the Canadian attack, COURCELETTE was taken. Report received of the success of the Canadians announced "Caterpillars". D/Battery took up position about 200 yards to the left rear of the other batteries. 240th & 243rd Brigades combined to form 48th Divisional group (Right) under command of Lt. Col. Went.	Q.P.B.?
OVILLERS	16/9/16		Nothing to report. B.C.s reconnoitred for O.Ps.	Q.P.B.?
OVILLERS	17/9/16		The group employed in Corps Artillery to thicken barrages where required. The CANADIANS reported holding MOUQUET FARM & the line running east along the railway line to COURCELETTE, including the Southern end of the ZOLLERN GRABEN.	Q.P.B.?
OVILLERS	18/9/16		Nothing to report.	Q.P.B.?
OVILLERS	19/9/16		A few shells fell round the H.Q. Qrs. of the 240th & 243rd Brigades one being a direct hit on the former, killing Major Q.D. Brown - O/C 240 & Lieut. W.R. Wybey - adjutant & wounding Capt. H. d'E. Vallancy A/243 & Capt. Laurence - M.O. 240 & Corpl. WR. Revers - D/240. Brigade Headquarters moved back to USNA REDOUBT.	Q.P.B.?
OVILLERS	20/9/16		Lieut. Hayes 87/240 took over command of A/241 vice Capt. Vallancy. Lieut. Ryan took over command of C/240 vice Major Brown. 2nd Lieut. Q.P. Brooke Jay is appointed adjutant vice Lieut. Wybey	
OVILLERS	21/9/16		Nothing to Report.	Q.P.B.?
OVILLERS	22/9/16			Q.P.B.?
OVILLERS	23/9/16		Canadians reported holding HIGH TRENCH, running North of MOUQUET FARM, having entered it they found it un-occupied.	Q.P.B.?

Army Form C. 2118

WAR DIARY
or
INTELLIGENCE SUMMARY
(Erase heading not required.)

240 Brigade R.F.A.
48th (S.M.) Division

Place	Date	Hour	Summary of Events and Information	Remarks and references to Appendices
OVILLERS.	24/9/16		Nothing to report.	R.A.B.D.
OVILLERS.	25/9/16		Enemy recaptured HIGH TRENCH & MOUQUET FARM.	R.A.D.
OVILLERS.	26/9/16		An attack was carried out at 12.35pm on the line running East from THIEPVAL to the North of COURCELETTE. The first two objectives were successfully reached as a line extending from the North of THIEPVAL along ZOLLERN TRENCH. Further progress made on our left STUFF REDOUBT (R21.c) captured	R.A.B.D.
OVILLERS.	27/9/16			R.A.B.D.
OVILLERS.	28/9/16		Attack made on SCHWABEN REDOUBT - North of THIEPVAL - & the larger part of it (R21d). Lieut. TIERNAN & two others (wounded) attack was made to take HESSIAN TRENCH reconnoitred for A & B. Batteries South of MOUQUET FARM & 'c' battery moved	R.A.B.D. R.A.D.
OVILLERS.	29/9/16		into new position North of POZIERES. Attack on HESSIAN TRENCH at 12.0 noon being successful through a portion of two redoubt was also retaken by the enemy counter attack. Northern side of SCHWABEN Artillery would be relieved by the 25th Divisional artillery, one section per Battery being relieved by them the same night. Attempts were made during the night to recapture portion of trench which had been lost, but entirely successful	R.A.B.D.
OVILLERS.	30/9/16		The attack during last night was not entirely successful & the position than morning is practically the same as yesterday. Operations were carried out on our left to recapture the STUFF REDOUBT which were only partly successful	R.A.B.D.

E.P.Brook Day
for Lieut. Colonel, R.F.A.
COMMANDING
240th (S.M.) Bde. R.F.A.

Vol 20

Volume 19   ORIGINAL

CONFIDENTIAL

WAR   DIARY

of

240th (S.M.) BRIGADE, R.F.A.

October
1916

G.P.Brooke-Taylor 2Lt.
for Lt.Col
Comdg.
240(SM)Bde RFA

Army Form C. 2118

WAR DIARY
or
INTELLIGENCE SUMMARY
(Erase heading not required.)

Instructions regarding War Diaries and Intelligence Summaries are contained in F.S. Regs., Part II. and the Staff Manual respectively. Title Pages will be prepared in manuscript.

Place	Date	Hour	Summary of Events and Information	Remarks and references to Appendices
ALBERT.	Oct 1st		Church Parade. B Battery took over four guns from B/82 Brigade.	
"	Oct 2nd	11 am	Very wet. Brigade moved from ALBERT. After a very wet march, arrived at WARLINCOURT, where it was necessary to draw over two hundred yards of very heavy stubble, to the wagon lines. Fixed up horse lines and bivouacs	
WARLINCOURT	Oct 3rd		Still very wet. Batteries remained at wagon line.	
"	Oct 4th		B Battery took over position of stripped guns of P/230.	
"	Oct 5th		D Battery moved into action in THE BLUFF, between FONQUEVILLERS and HEBUTERNE. Two guns of D Battery were condemned, with cracks in the breech, so were left at I.O.M. SOUASTRE. B Battery registered.	
"	Oct 6th		B Battery prepared position for section of 4/230 which was attached to them.	
"	Oct 7th		D Battery moved to new position near CHATEAU LA HAIE. Brigade Wagon Lines moved from WARLINCOURT to SOUASTRE. Brigade H.Q. moved to SOUASTRE.	

Army Form C. 2118

WAR DIARY
or
INTELLIGENCE SUMMARY

(Erase heading not required.)

Instructions regarding War Diaries and Intelligence Summaries are contained in F. S. Regs., Part II. and the Staff Manual respectively. Title Pages will be prepared in manuscript.

Place	Date	Hour	Summary of Events and Information	Remarks and references to Appendices
SOUASTRE	Oct 8th		B Battery registered. D Battery improved pits taken over yesterday.	
"	" 9th		B Battery sent a gun to Ordnance. D Battery continued work at gun position, and at the O.P. in THORPE STREET.	
"	" 10th		D Battery still at work on gun position and O.P. and received one gun from Ordnance.	
"	" 11th		B Battery registered. O.P. "O" in THORPE ST. shelled by 150 m.m. How. Trench in front of O.P. badly damaged but O.P. untouched.	
"	" 12th		D Battery started work on new O.P. in YANKEE STREET.	
"	" 13th		B Battery were wire cutting. D Battery continued work at O.P.	
"	" 14th		B Battery had gun from Ordnance and sent another in for overhaul. D Battery continued work at O.P.	
"	" 15th		Nothing to report	
"	" 16th			
"	" 17th		B Battery received gun from Ordnance and sent another in for overhaul.	

Army Form C. 2118

WAR DIARY
or
INTELLIGENCE SUMMARY
(Erase heading not required.)

Place	Date	Hour	Summary of Events and Information	Remarks and references to Appendices
SOUASTRE	Oct. 18th		Re-organisation of Divisional Artillery. 243rd Brigade split up between 240 and 241 Brigades. A/243 and C/C/243 joined 290 Brigade - B/243 going to A/240, B/243 going to B/290 and ½/243 going to C/290. The Brigade now consists of 3- 6 gun 18-Pdr Batteries and one 4-gun 4.5 How Battery. Major CONSTANTINE of 243 Brigade took over command of C/290 Battery. B and C/290 Battery moved their horse lines to standings at WARLINCOURT; wagons being parked at HENU.	
"	" 19th		D Battery moved into position they left on 7th October	
"	" 20th		Nothing to report	
"	" 21st		Nothing to report. Heavy ground mist, which rendered observation impossible	
"	" 22nd		Heavy rain. D Battery shelled with tear shell and poison gas shell. Major E.W. Todd APWO received D.S.O.	
"	" 23rd		Enemy lines invisible owing to mist. D Battery shelled with gas shell - one man being slightly gassed otherwise no damage.	

Army Form C. 2118

WAR DIARY
or
INTELLIGENCE SUMMARY
(Erase heading not required.)

Instructions regarding War Diaries and Intelligence Summaries are contained in F. S. Regs., Part II. and the Staff Manual respectively. Title Pages will be prepared in manuscript.

Place	Date	Hour	Summary of Events and Information	Remarks and references to Appendices
SOUASTRE	24th Oct		Observation impossible owing to mist.	
	25th Oct.		A&C Batterys registering. D Battery engaged on counter battery work, but very little firing, owing to small allotment of ammunition	
	26th Oct.		A B & C Batteries registering. D Battery fired 500 rounds counter battery	
	27th Oct.		All Batteries registering	
	28th Oct.		All Batteries registered. 0/240 did night firing.	
	29th Oct.		All Batteries registered. B & D Batteries heavily shelled by 150 mm and gas shell. G/240 did night firing	
	30th Oct.		All Batteries registered. A & B Batteries were night firing	
	31st Oct.		Nothing to report.	

G. P. Brooke Taylor

1875 Wt. W593/826 1,000,000 4/15 J.B.C. & A. A.D.S.S./Forms/C. 2118.

CONFIDENTIAL ORIGINAL

VOLUME 20

WAR DIARY
of
240th (S.M.) BRIGADE, R.F.A.

for the period

1st November, 1916 to 30th November 1916.

for Lieut-Colonel,
Commanding,
240th (S.M.) Brigade, R.F.A.

Army Form C. 2118.

WAR DIARY
or
INTELLIGENCE SUMMARY.
(Erase heading not required.)

Instructions regarding War Diaries and Intelligence Summaries are contained in F. S. Regs, Part II. and the Staff Manual respectively. Title pages will be prepared in manuscript.

Place	Date	Hour	Summary of Events and Information	Remarks and references to Appendices
SOUASTRE	1/11/16		Very wet. A few registering rounds fired. D/280 Battery being attacked by Heavy Artillery Group fired 300 rounds counter battery.	
"	2/11/16		Night of 1-2nd B/Battery did night firing. Wet. Visibility poor. All batteries did a little registering during the afternoon	
"	3/11/16		Very windy but fine. Considerable aerial activity in spite of high wind. D Battery engaged several hostile batteries. Registering was rendered difficult owing to wind. M. of R. A. inspected O.P. of the Brigade.	
"	4/11/16		Work continued on positions	
"	5/11/16		Nothing to report.	
"	6/11/16		A.B. and C Batteries registered. D Battery did counter Battery work. Working parties were fired on by A Battery.	
"	7/11/16		Very wet - nothing to report	
"	8/11/16		Enemy not long parties fired on. A lineman of D Battery was wounded in FONQUEVILLERS.	
"	9/11/16		A/Battery very heavily shelled by 5.9". One gun was destroyed and considerable damage done to small equipment, but there were no casualties. Very little of our own firing	

WAR DIARY
or
INTELLIGENCE SUMMARY
(Erase heading not required.)

Army Form C. 2118.

Place	Date	Hour	Summary of Events and Information	Remarks and references to Appendices
SOUASTRE	10/11/16		Improvement in the weather. A Battery were given orders to move their position owing to the shelling yesterday. Brigade checked "aerial barrage". Trench mortars active in GOMMECOURT upon which D Battery retaliated.	
"	11/11/16		Nothing to report.	
"	12/11/16		Very good day for registering. Batteries registered points in connection with operations for 13th.	
"	13/11/16		An attack was launched by the Divisions south of us on the line from SERRE to SCHWABEN REDOUBT with considerable success. The Division immediately on our right was unable to gain ground but BEAUMONT HAMEL and ST PIERRE DIVION were taken and a defensive line established from north of BEAUMONT HAMEL south-east to SCHWABEN REDOUBT.	
	14/11/16		The line advanced as far as BEAUCOURT. Total prisoners reported captured amounted to 6,000.	
	15/11/16		Nothing to report.	
	16/11/16		ANCRE TRENCH reported captured, and position established in BOIS d'HOLLANDE.	

Army Form C. 2118.

WAR DIARY
or
INTELLIGENCE SUMMARY.
(Erase heading not required.)

Instructions regarding War Diaries and Intelligence Summaries are contained in F.S. Regs., Part II. and the Staff Manual respectively. Title pages will be prepared in manuscript.

Place	Date	Hour	Summary of Events and Information	Remarks and references to Appendices
SOUASTRE	17/11/16		Right Group 48th Divisional Artillery became attached to 46th Division and the Brigade became Right Group. 48th Divisional Artillery and 242nd Brigade became Centre Group. Right Group Zones remained the same.	
	18/11/16		Fall of snow. Nothing to Report.	
	19/11/16		Nothing to Report.	
	20/11/16		147th Infantry Brigade carried out a raid on the enemy trenches on the western edge of GOMMECOURT PARK. The wire was cut with a Bangalor torpedo by the artillery was used for a protective barrage. The enterprise was successful and several of the enemy were killed and dugouts destroyed. Our loss the loss of only two men killed. No prisoners were taken by either side.	
	21/11/16		Enemy Artillery very active along GOMMECOURT front.	
	22/11/16		Nothing to report	
	23/11/16		Rear positions reconnoitered by O.C. and Battery Commanders.	
	24/11/16		Nothing to report	
	25/11/16		Nothing to report	

Army Form C. 2118.

WAR DIARY
or
INTELLIGENCE SUMMARY.
(Erase heading not required.)

Instructions regarding War Diaries and Intelligence Summaries are contained in F. S. Regs., Part II. and the Staff Manual respectively. Title pages will be prepared in manuscript.

Place	Date	Hour	Summary of Events and Information	Remarks and references to Appendices
SOUASTRE	26/11/16		Nothing to report	A.A.
PAS	27/11/16		48th Div. Artillery were relieved in action by 49th Div. Artillery and batteries returned to their wagon lines at PAS.	A.A.
"	28/11/16		Guns received from 49th Div. Artillery and preparations made for march.	A.A.
"	29/11/16		The Brigade marched from PAS via DOULLENS and FROHEN-LE-GRAND and then to REMAISNIL	A.A.
"	30/11/16		The remainder of 48th Div. Artillery joined the Brigade in the MÉZEROLLES district	A.A.

CONFIDENTIAL.   ORIGINAL

WAR DIARY
of

240th (S.M.) BRIGADE, R.F.A.

for the period

1st DECEMBER 1916   to   31st DECEMBER 1916.

VOLUME   21.

----

for Lt-Colonel,
Commanding
240th (S.M.) Brigade, R.F.A.

Army Form C. 2118.

WAR DIARY
or
INTELLIGENCE SUMMARY.
(Erase heading not required.)

Instructions regarding War Diaries and Intelligence Summaries are contained in F.S. Regs., Part II. and the Staff Manual respectively. Title pages will be prepared in manuscript.

Place	Date	Hour	Summary of Events and Information	Remarks and references to Appendices
TALMAS	1/12/16		The Brigade continued its march to TALMAS and remained one night	
BEHENCOURT	2/12/16		The march continued to BEHENCOURT.	
"	3/12/16		95th Brigade reconnoitred positions to be taken over in action.	
	4/12/16		Battery commanders and one section per battery marched via ALBERT and CONTALMAISON to take up positions between HIGH WOOD and MARTIN PUICH.	
	5/12/16		The remainder of the Brigade proceeded to these positions and relieved 103 Bde R.F.A. Wagon lines were established on the west side of CONTALMAISON. The Brigade zone extended from M10c southwards to the Bute de Warlencourt - M17a. Brigade H.Q. were established in cemetery at BAZANTIN LE PETIT.	
BAZANTIN LE PETIT	6/12/16		Registration	
"	7/12/16		Observation impossible owing to mist.	
"	8/12/16		Observation impossible owing to mist.	
"	9/12/16		Too misty to observe Nothing to report.	
"	10/12/16		Lightshower. Registration carried out.	

Army Form C. 2118.

WAR DIARY
or
INTELLIGENCE SUMMARY
(Erase heading not required.)

Instructions regarding War Diaries and Intelligence Summaries are contained in F. S. Regs., Part II. and the Staff Manual respectively. Title pages will be prepared in manuscript.

Place	Date	Hour	Summary of Events and Information	Remarks and references to Appendices
BAZANTIN LE PETIT	11/12/16		Registration. Bursts of fire each night on tracks and approaches north of WARLENCOURT	1/12/16
	12/12/16		Nothing to report.	1/12/16
	13/12/16		A Battery wagon line moved back behind ALBERT to W27c. Ammunition supply for A Battery was undertaken by D/290.	1/12/16
	14/12/16		Bombardment carried out on our right by 1st Division.	1/12/16
	15/12/16		C Battery moved their wagon line behind ALBERT to W27c. New ammunition supply was taken over by B/290. Brigade zone altered to extend from M10c & M6.5 to M17a O.6 to correspond with Battalion front.	1/12/16
	16/12/16		Nothing to report	1/12/16
	17/12/16		15th Div. Headquarters relieved 48th Div. Headquarters who returned to rest in ALBERT.	1/12/16
	18/12/16		Nothing to report	1/12/16
	19/12/16		Orders were received by 15th Divisional Artillery to expend up to Brigade allotment i.e. 650 rds 18-Pdr and 200 rounds 4.5" Hows per day.	1/12/16

Army Form C. 2118.

WAR DIARY
or
INTELLIGENCE SUMMARY.
(Erase heading not required.)

Place	Date	Hour	Summary of Events and Information	Remarks and references to Appendices
BALENTIN LE PETIT	20/12/16		Brigade gone again changed back to extend from QUARRY M17a 06 to M10d 14	1/E
	21/12/16		2nd Brigade combined with 72nd Bde to form the Right Sub Group under the command of O.C. 72nd Bde	1/E
	22/12/16		Organized shoots round for every day	1/E
	23/12/16		Nothing to report	1/E
	24/12/16		Nothing to report	1/E
	25/12/16		Normal activity. 3 salvos fired during the morning simultaneously by the artillery of the Corps	1/E
	26/12/16		Nothing to report	1/E
	27/12/16		Nothing to report	1/E
	28/12/16		Concentration scheme practised.	1/E
	29/12/16		Concentration scheme. Orders received of the relief of the Brigade by 24th Brigade.	1/E
	30/12/16		Battery bombardeur 241 Bde. and half battery came up. Relief of Brigade complete. Batteries remaining: battery came up to take over	1/E
	31/12/16		Marched back to BEHENCOURT via ALBERT and FRANVILLERS. Bde H.Q. remained one night in ALBERT.	1/E

CONFIDENTIAL   ORIGINAL

Vol 23

W A R   D I A R Y

    for the period
1st January to 31st January 1917.

    Volume   22

240 th (S.M.) Brigade, R.F.A.

                                  Lieut. & Adjutant,
240th (S.M.) Brigade, R.F.A.

CONFIDENTIAL

Army Form C. 2118.

WAR DIARY
or
INTELLIGENCE SUMMARY.
(Erase heading not required.)

Place	Date	Hour	Summary of Events and Information	Remarks and references to Appendices
BEHENCOURT	1-1-17		Brigade headquarters moved from ALBERT and formed the battery at BEHENCOURT	
	2-1-17		Cleaning up	
	3-1-17		Conference of Battery Commanders with 60C Division	
	4-7-17		Tactical Exercises for Battery Commanders with 60 6 Division	
	6pm		Extracts from New Year's List of Honours. Captain D DAVIDSON (RAMC) awarded military Cross. 25166 B.S.M. S/SM MOSS, RG awarded D.C.M. 51902 Sergt. qBSM BLACKMAN.G.W and 653 Arm. S/Sergt MARKEY L.E awarded M.S.M.	
	5-1-17		Routine Parades - Gun Drill, marching circle etc.	
	6-1-17		Bombing Lecture for Officers and Telephonists	
	7-1-17		Voluntary Church Parade. Bombing Lecture.	
	8-1-17		Bombing lecture. Lecture by CRA in the evening. The Brigade was inspected in dismounted order by G.O.C. Division	
	9-1-17		Lecture by Medical Officer. Routine parades daily. Gun drill, marching drill and riding.	

WAR DIARY
INTELLIGENCE SUMMARY

Army Form C. 2118.

Place	Date	Hour	Summary of Events and Information	Remarks and references to Appendices
BEHENCOURT	10-1-17		Lecture by Lieut. W. O. RYAN.	
"	11-1-17		Routine Parades	
"	12-1-17		Preparation for relief of 242 Bde in the line	
"	13-1-17		½ Battery A/240, ½ Battery C/240 and ½ Battery D/240 went up to take over positions west of MARTIN PUICH from B, A and D/242 respectively. Remaining ½ Batteries and Brigade H.Q. completed the relief at noon.	
CONTALMAISON VILLA	14-1-17		Wagon lines of C and D/240 established close to ALBERT and the whole of lines A/240 remained at BEHENCOURT together with the whole of B Battery. 240 Brigade together with 72 Brigade formed Left Sub Group of Left Artillery Group. (15th Div. Arty) The position of A/240 shelled with 5.9. and lachrymatory shell during the night. Casualties one man slightly gassed, one gun out of action damage to muzzle. The 48th Divisional Artillery was again reorganised 242 Bde becoming Army troops and 240 and 241 Brigades remaining as Divisional Artillery with the addition of one section Howitzers each from C/242 Battery.	

Army Form C. 2118.

WAR DIARY
or
INTELLIGENCE SUMMARY.
(Erase heading not required.)

Instructions regarding War Diaries and Intelligence Summaries are contained in F. S. Regs., Part II. and the Staff Manual respectively. Title pages will be prepared in manuscript.

Place	Date	Hour	Summary of Events and Information	Remarks and references to Appendices
CONTAL MAISON VILLA	15-1-17		Registration. Enemy artillery very active.	
	16-1-17		Very misty.	
	17-1-17		Usual daily programme on GALWITZ TRENCH and tracks in rear.	
	18-1-17		During the night 17/18 C Battery position heavily shelled with all calibres including lachrymatory shell. Breveille engagement of action. Two N.C.O.'s were damaged. A and D Batteries each received 2 guns from their positions and took them to I.O.M. workshops for overhaul.	
	19-1-17		A Battery withdrew another section and took the guns to IOM	
	20-1-17		A Battery withdrew their last two guns and vacated their position.	
	21-1-17		Personnel of C and D Batteries were relieved by 72nd Brigade and returned to their wagon lines.	
	22-1-17		C + D Batteries marched to BAVINCOURT. Brigade HQ were evacuated and Headquarters staff marched to BAVINCOURT.	
BAVINCOURT	23-1-17		Nothing to report.	
	24-1-17		Routine parades. Bivouacs cleaning etc.	

WAR DIARY
or
INTELLIGENCE SUMMARY.
(Erase heading not required.)

Army Form C. 2118.

Place	Date	Hour	Summary of Events and Information	Remarks and references to Appendices
BAVINCOURT	25/1/17		Brigade and Battery Commanders and Reconnaissance Officers went forward to the new area in front of PERONNE, to reconnoitre their positions.	1/WD
	26/1/17		The Brigade marched via PONT NOYELLES, DAUORS to FOUILLOY and billeted there.	1/26
FOUILLOY	27/1/17		Nothing to report	1/27
	28/1/17		The Brigade and Battery Commanders reconnoitred the position in the forward area. Battery positions for Brigade were situated east of FLAUCOURT covering a portion of front which included PERONNE.	1/28
	29/1/17		Each Battery sent up a working party to prepare their positions	1/29
	30/1/17		Reconnaissance of wagon line.	1/30
	31/1/17		Reconnaissance of O.P. by Brigade and Battery Commanders.	1/31

CONFIDENTIAL   ORIGINAL

Vol 24

WAR   DIARY

of

240th. (S.M.) BRIGADE, R.F.A.

FOR THE PERIOD 1st to 28th FEBRUARY, 1917

VOLUME 24.

-- -- -- -- -- -- -- -- -- -- --

G.P.Brooke Taylor
for LIEUT. COLONEL, R.F.A.
COMMANDING
240th (S.M.) Bde. R.F.A.

Army Form C. 2118.

WAR DIARY
or
INTELLIGENCE SUMMARY.
(Erase heading not required.)

Instructions regarding War Diaries and Intelligence Summaries are contained in F. S. Regs., Part II. and the Staff Manual respectively. Title pages will be prepared in manuscript.

Place	Date	Hour	Summary of Events and Information	Remarks and references to Appendices
FOUILLOY	1st Feb 1917		Nothing to report.	
"	2d.		1 Bay Batteries moved up to Wagon Line positions in CAPPY.	G.P.S.?
CAPPY	3d.		The guns of 1/2 Batteries moved up into positions east of FLAUCOURT relieving the French Batteries in action there. Remaining 1/2 Batteries of Bat. moved up to Wagon Lines in CAPPY.	G.P.S.? Remainder Batteries P.R.?
"	4th.		Brigade H.Q. and remainder of Batteries moved up into action. French 1/2 Batteries did not move out. The enemy raided our trenches at two points opposite BIACHES and BARLEUX after a bombardment of the trenches. They were repulsed leaving a few prisoners. 143 and 144 Brigades suffered casualties to the extent of about 100. Battery positions were shelled with tear gas.	G.P.S.?
FLAUCOURT	5th		All guns were registered on barrage lines	
"	6th.		Remainder of French guns were withdrawn in the early morning and the command of the front was taken over by the English.	G.P.S.? G.P.S.?
"	7th.		48th Div. Arty. split up to form two Sub Groups, Right and Left, under the command of Lt. Col. A.B. Escourt and Lt. Col. The Lord Wynford respectively.	G.P.S.?

Army Form C. 2118.

WAR DIARY
or
INTELLIGENCE SUMMARY.
(Erase heading not required.)

Instructions regarding War Diaries and Intelligence Summaries are contained in F.S. Regs., Part II. and the Staff Manual respectively. Title pages will be prepared in manuscript.

Place	Date	Hour	Summary of Events and Information	Remarks and references to Appendices
FLAUCOURT	7/2/17		Left Sub Group consisted of A/240 Battery and A/B.C and D Batteries of 241 Brigade covering the front from the river to just south of MAISONETTE. Casualties 2/Lieut J.H. WOODLANDS, R.E attached, wounded. One other rank slightly wounded.	G.R.O
"	8-2-17		Registration.	G.R.O.
"	9-2-17		Hostile activity normal	G.R.O.
"	10-2-17		The zone of the Left Infantry Brigade was slightly decreased running only as far SOUTH to BURGER TRENCH. A/240 and C/241 were transferred to the Right Sub Group and the front of the Left Brigade was covered only by A/15 - D/241.	G.R.O.
"	11-2-17		Nothing to report	G.R.O.
"	12-2-17		Observation clear, hostile trench mortar emplacement at I.26.w.15.77 shelled by D/241, and men were seen to vacate the trench closely.	G.R.O.
	13-2-17		Nothing to report.	G.R.O.
	14-2-17		Nothing to report.	G.R.B.
	15-2-17		Nothing to report.	G.R.O.

WAR DIARY
or
INTELLIGENCE SUMMARY.
(Erase heading not required.)

Army Form C. 2118.

Place	Date	Hour	Summary of Events and Information	Remarks and references to Appendices
FLAUCOURT	16-2-17		Nothing to report	(q.P.R.?)
"	17-2-17		Nothing to report.	(q.P.R.?)
"	18-2-17		Enemy artillery more active than usual	(q.P.R.?)
"	19-2-17		Wire cutting commenced, but owing to bad light did not last long.	(q.P.R.?)
"	20-2-17		Nothing to report. Observation very difficult owing to fog	(q.P.R.?)
"	21-2-17		Wire cutting continued and considerable damage was done.	(q.P.R.?)
"	22-2-17		Wire cutting continued and gaps already made kept open.	(q.P.R.?)
"	23-2-17		Enemy was kept up on Tow-path and MEHARI Trench at irregular intervals throughout the day, also gaps made previously in the Wire were kept open. Wire cutting and registration impossible owing to low visibility. Harassers fired on BOSTON Trench.	(q.P.R.?)
		8pm	Right Company of Right Battalion sent up S.O.S. Signal. They were being heavily shelled. Barrage fire was opened at once. This was stopped almost immediately, as no enemy were observed to be advancing.	
"	24-2-17		Light improved, still poor for observation. Fire was kept on approaches to enemy lines throughout the day. Wire cutting impossible.	(q.P.R.?)

WAR DIARY
or
INTELLIGENCE SUMMARY.

(Erase heading not required.)

Army Form C. 2118.

Place	Date	Hour	Summary of Events and Information	Remarks and references to Appendices
Flaucourt	24.2.17	6 am	Infantry asked for retaliation, as they were being shelled by minenwerfer. Fire was opened and the minnies were successfully silenced. From today Group was relieved of keeping open gaps in the wire at night by the Infantry Machine Gun Officer.	G.P.B.?
"	25.2.17		Light good for observation. A/240 continued wire cutting. #3rd Divisional Artillery was formed into three groups of which 240 Bde was Centre Sub Group.	G.P.B.?
"	26.2.17		Very good light for observation purposes. A/240 continued wire cutting. Hostile working parties were observed and dispersed. A raid on the enemy trenches was arranged with 145 Inf. Brigade, in which Centre Sub Group in conjunction with Right Sub Group took part. The enemy's trenches were not penetrated owing to the strength of his wire.	G.P.B.?
"	27.2.17		A Battery continued wire cutting with satisfactory results.	G.P.B.?
"	28.2.17		At 1am and 6.25 am the Group took part in a bombardment of the enemy lines.	G.P.B.?

CONFIDENTIAL.   ORIGINAL.

Vol 25

WAR   DIARY

of

240th. (S.M.) BRIGADE", R.F.A.

FOR THE PERIOD 1st to 31st MARCH, 1917.

VOLUME   25.

G. P. Alcoke Taylor 2L
for Lieut. Colonel
Commanding
240 (SM) Brigade. R.F.A.

WAR DIARY
or
INTELLIGENCE SUMMARY.
(Erase heading not required.)

Army Form C. 2118.

Place	Date	Hour	Summary of Events and Information	Remarks and references to Appendices
FLAUCOURT	1st March 17		Two 18 Pdr Batteries did considerable damage to the enemy wire.	G.P.R.O.
"	2nd		4.5" How bombarded points as arranged in Bombardment scheme. Visibility bad. Infantry asked for retaliation.	G.P.R.O.
"	3rd		Visibility bad. B/240 Battery had one other rank killed.	G.P.R.O.
"	4th		Clear. Enemy aeroplanes very active - one flying over FLAUCOURT and Apero Battery position very low.	G.P.R.O.
"	5th		Nothing to report.	G.P.R.O.
"	6th		Light good. C.O. registered most batteries for raid in conjunction with 1/4 Royal Berks Group took part in concentration on Centre Sector Scheme.	G.P.R.O.
"	7th		C.O. continued registration of batteries. Raid carried out on enemy trenches finding front line empty the operation was repeated, support lines being entered, two prisoners were captured.	G.P.R.O.
"	8th	"	Light bad for observation until late in the afternoon. Wires were observed in enemy's lines and in PERSONNE.	G.P.R.O.
"	9th		Nothing to report.	G.P.R.O.
"	10th		Batteries took part in bombardment scheme on enemy trenches	G.P.R.O.

WAR DIARY
or
INTELLIGENCE SUMMARY.
(Erase heading not required.)

Army Form C. 2118.

Place	Date	Hour	Summary of Events and Information	Remarks and references to Appendices
FLAUCOURT	11/3/17		All batteries took part in bombardment of enemys trenches. Registration and wire cutting was carried on throughout the day. Observation good.	G.P.B.?
"	12-3-17		Registration continued	G.P.B.?
"	13.3.17		Nothing to report.	G.P.B.?
"	14-3-17		Nothing to report.	G.P.B.?
"	15-3-17		Nothing to report.	G.P.B.?
"	16-3-17		Nothing to report.	G.P.B.?
"	17-3-17		During the night 16/17 144th Brigade made a raid on the enemy trenches meeting little opposition and capturing 1st 2nd and 3rd lines of defence. BARLEUX, BIACHES and ETERPIGNY were occupied later on the day. Posts were established up to the RIVER SOMME. Battery commanders reconnoitred positions with a view to moving on 18th.	G.P.B.?
	18/3/17 19/3/17 20/3/17		} Nothing to report.	G.P.B.?
	21/3/17		½ H.Q. C and D Batteries moved with Mobile force across the RIVER	G.P.B.?

WAR DIARY
or
INTELLIGENCE SUMMARY.
(Erase heading not required.)

Army Form C. 2118.

Place	Date	Hour	Summary of Events and Information	Remarks and references to Appendices
FLAUCOURT	22/3/17		...with the intention of finding touch with enemy. The mobile force marched to DOINGT.	G.P.B.?
"	22/3/17		The remainder of H.Q. A and B Batteries moved back from FLAUCOURT to CAPPY, being prepared to move out at a moment's notice	G.P.B.?
DOINGT	23/3/17		C Battery moved to CARTIGNY. D Battery and H.Q. to COURCELLES. A and B batteries remained CAPPY. Nothing to report	G.P.B.?
COURCELLES	24/3/17			G.P.B.?
"	25/3/17		D Battery sent one section to shell ROISEL and helped cavalry to clear TINCOURT WOOD. 5/H.Q. A & B Batteries marched from CAPPY to A12 BOU RT-15-1790T. B Battery went into action in the village.	G.P.B.?
	26/3/17		C and D Batteries co-operated with 8th and Bucks L.I. and Indian Cavalry in the capture of ROISEL. A and B Battery went into action near TEMPLEUX.	G.P.B.?
	27/3/17		C and D Batteries co-operated with Horse Artillery and Cavalry in the capture of Villers Faucon. Headquarters marched to TINCOURT. A and B Batteries came out of action near TEMPLEUX	G.P.B.? G.P.B.? G.P.B.?
	28/3/17			

WAR DIARY
or
INTELLIGENCE SUMMARY.
(Erase heading not required.)

Army Form C. 2118.

Place	Date	Hour	Summary of Events and Information	Remarks and references to Appendices
TINCOURT	29/3/17		and marched to TINCOURT where they both went into action.	e.P.R.?
"	30/3/17		Nothing to report.	e.P.R.?
"	"		B and D Batteries moved 1 gun each into the vicinity of VILLERS FAUCON. Remainder of D Battery guns joined the one gun later on the day, and C Battery moved into action further forward. Our Infantry attacked ST. EMILIE at 4 o'clock in the afternoon, capturing the village and during large numbers of the enemy into the open beyond. 2nd Lieutenant P.T.W. YIRRELL was wounded in action and subsequently died in hospital.	
"	31/3/17		Headquarters moved forward into SAULCOURT WOOD. The Division on our right attacked the high ground on the right including HESBECOURT, so making it possible to move guns forward on the right.	e.P.R.?

E.P. Rutherford Lieut
for Lieut- Col. Comdg.
240 (S.M) Brigade R.F.A.

CONFIDENTIAL.   VOLUME. 26

ORIGNAL.

Vol 26

WAR   DIARY

OF THE

240th (S. M.) BRIGADE, R. F. A.

FOR   THE   PERIOD,

1 st.   to   the   30 th.   APRIL, 1917.

----

for   D.P. Morgan /Lt
LIEUT. COLONEL, R.F.A.
COMMANDING
240th (S.M.) BDE. R.F.A.

CONFIDENTIAL

From — Officer COMMANDING
240th (S.M.) BDE. R.F.A.

To H.Q.
    48th D.A.

Herewith Original copy of WAR DIARY Volume 26, of the 240th (S.M.) Brigade, R.F.A. for the period 1st to 30th April 1917.

D.P. Morgan 2/Lt
for LIEUT. COLONEL, R.F.A.
COMMANDING
240th (S.M.) BDE. R.F.A.

1st May 1917

CONFIDENTIAL

Army Form C. 2118.

WAR DIARY
or
INTELLIGENCE SUMMARY.
(Erase heading not required.)

Place	Date	Hour	Summary of Events and Information	Remarks and references to Appendices
SAULCOURT WOOD.	1st April/17	At 6am	At 6am the Brigade assisted 144th Infy Brigade in an attack on EPEHY, which was successful. 12 Prisoners and 3 machine guns were captured. A Battery moved to a position forward. The detached section of D Battery joined the remainder of the Battery.	D.P.П.
"	2nd		At 6pm. A and D Batteries cooperated with the Infantry in an attack on RONSSOY. The attack failed. B Battery and 2 guns of C Battery moved into positions further forward.	D.P.П
"	3rd		Registration of RONSSOY carried out, in preparation of second attack on this village. C and D Batteries moved into positions further forward in the vicinity of ST EMILIE. Field Marshall Sir Douglas HAIG. Commander in Chief, congratulated the GOC Divison, on the work done by the 48th Div. during the past few weeks.	D.P.П
"	4th		Owing to a heavy snowstorm and thick mist observation was impossible.	D.P.П
"	5th		The Brigade co-operated with 145th Brigade in an attack on the villages of RONSSOY, LEMPIRE and BASSÉ BOULOGNE. The attack was successful.	D.P.П

Army Form C. 2118.

WAR DIARY
or
INTELLIGENCE SUMMARY.
(Erase heading not required.)

Place	Date	Hour	Summary of Events and Information	Remarks and references to Appendices
SAULCOURT WOOD	6th April 17		A and B Batteries moved forward to new position. C Battery detached section rejoined the Battery.	DPN
"			Headquarters moved forward to ST EMILIE.	DPN
ST EMILIE	7th		D Battery moved one section to forward position A/240 and one section D/240 assisted 59th Div. in an attack on Cross Roads in F.29.b. The attack was unsuccessful.	DPN
"	8th		Commanding Officer reconnoitred O.P. and decided on position of Brigade O.P. A Battery cut wire at L.10.b.	DPN
		8.30pm 9.30pm	B Batteries shelled enemy outpost line at slow rate of fire. D Battery moved 4 guns to new forward position in F.13.c.4.2.	DPN
	9th		A and B Batteries of 211 Brigade were attached to this Brigade. Battery Commanders of A and B/211 reconnoitred positions and O.P's and Batteries moved into action in the evening in the neighbourhood of TEMPEUX LE GUERARD and BOUROUXWOOD. One section D/240 and 18 Pdr fired on approach to TOM BOIS FARM and roads in the neighbourhood thereof.	DPN

Army Form C. 2118.

WAR DIARY
or
INTELLIGENCE SUMMARY.
(Erase heading not required.)

Instructions regarding War Diaries and Intelligence Summaries are contained in F. S. Regs., Part II. and the Staff Manual respectively. Title pages will be prepared in manuscript.

Place	Date	Hour	Summary of Events and Information	Remarks and references to Appendices
ST.E.MIHIEL	10/4/17		During the morning 18 Pdrs registered on German front line in preparation for an attack. Slow "snip" fire was kept on enemy trenches until midnight and until 4.30 am when our Infantry advanced and captured cross sunken roads in F.29.b.	D.P.D.
"	11/4/17		Two guns of B/240 moved to new position and evening of 11th	D.P.D.
"	12/4/17		B Battery cut wire at F.17.b and 23.b. Batteries registered in preparation for an attack on enemy trenches running from TOMBOIS FARM to sunken cross roads in F.29.b. Batteries maintained a dropping fire at a slow rate along the German trenches during the night until 3.30 am on 13/4/17, when the Infantry assisted with two Battalions - 7th Worcesters and 4th Gloster - and obtained all objectives capturing 4 prisoners and a machine gun. Our casualties were light. An enemy counter attack was dispersed by our fire.	D.P.D.
"	13/4/17			
"	14/4/17		C Battery wagon line moved to the neighbourhood of ST.E.MIHIEL. Capt. McLeod took over the command of B/240 Bty. All the debilitated horses were collected and kept apart under the order of the Veterinary Officer	D.P.D.

WAR DIARY
or
INTELLIGENCE SUMMARY.
(Erase heading not required.)

Army Form C. 2118.

Place	Date	Hour	Summary of Events and Information	Remarks and references to Appendices
ST EMILIE	15/4/17		A and B/211 Batteries registered during the day. is assist the 59th Div. in an attack on VILLARET. The Infantry attacked about 9.30pm and obtained all objectives.	D.P.11
"	16/4/17		During the night 15/16 C/290 moved forward to a position in RONSSOY WOOD. A/240 also moved forward and B/211 occupied a new position in F.2.a.	D.P.11
"	17/4/17		During the day Batteries registered in preparation for an attack on TOMBOIS FARM and GILLEMONT FARM and the high ground beyond.	D.P.11
		11.30pm	The Infantry attacked the Left Battalion gaining TOMBOIS FARM. The enemy heavily barraged the Right Batt'n. so that they were unable to leave their trenches	
"	18/4/17	6.45am	The enemy counter attacked TOMBOIS FARM approaching along VENDHUILE ROAD. This was dispersed by our curtain fire. One other rank of A/240 Battery was slightly wounded but remained at duty. B/240 cable wires in front of GILLEMONT FARM	D.P.11

Army Form C. 2118.

WAR DIARY
or
INTELLIGENCE SUMMARY.
(Erase heading not required.)

Instructions regarding War Diaries and Intelligence Summaries are contained in F. S. Regs., Part II. and the Staff Manual respectively. Title pages will be prepared in manuscript.

Place	Date	Hour	Summary of Events and Information	Remarks and references to Appendices
BEMMLIE	18/4/17		The proposed operations on GILLEMONT FARM were postponed. During the afternoon batteries registered for a further attack on GILLEMONT FARM.	D.P.N.
"	19/4/17		Infantry advanced at 7.30 p.m. but owing to heavy machine gun fire were unable to take the farm.	D.P.N.
"	20/4/17		A/240 moved 1 gun forward to a position in F.28.a.5.2	D.P.N.
"	21/4/17		A/240 moved one section forward during the night to cut wire in front of GILLEMONT FARM. The section occupied a position about F.22.b.3.2.	D.P.N.
"	22/4/17		Batteries fired practice barrages for a further attack on GILLEMONT FARM and "THE KNOLL". Brigade O.P. selected at F.16.a.0.6.	D.P.N.
"	23/4/17		A/241 moved remaining guns into action in the early morning. C.R.A. observed barrages. M.G.R.A. visited O.P. and some battery positions	D.P.N.
"	24/4/17		Batteries carried out final registration for the attack on GILLEMONT FARM and THE KNOLL during the afternoon	D.P.N.
		11 p.m.	The 144 Inf Bde attacked GILLEMONT FARM and THE KNOLL with two	1

T2134. Wt. W708—776. 500000. 4/15. Sir J. C. & S.

WAR DIARY
or
INTELLIGENCE SUMMARY.
(Erase heading not required.)

Army Form C. 2118.

Place	Date	Hour	Summary of Events and Information	Remarks and references to Appendices
ST EMILIE			Battalions, the 7th Worc on the right and 4th Glo. on the left. The 7th Worc captured the farm against heavy opposition. The 4th Glo. obtained a footing on THE KNOLL but subsequently had to withdraw.	DPM
"	25/4/17	6.45am	enemy counterattacked GILLEMONT FARM in force - estimated enemy force 1 Battalion - these were broken up by our barrage	DPM
		8.45am	enemy again counterattacked, and again at 9.30 am, in the former case being driven off by M.G. fire and in the latter our barrage was called for and the enemy were dispersed. Sniping fire was carried out with considerable success during the day	DPM
"	26/4/17		During the nights 25/26 Batteries kept up slow rate of fire on villages and approaches to GILLEMONT FARM. 9 and 8/211 registered barrage to assist 59th Div. in their attack on the QUARRIES, the RAILWAY bank 15 of HARGICOURT. German trenches and COLOGNE FARM in L.b.c. Zero hour for this	DPM

WAR DIARY
or
INTELLIGENCE SUMMARY.
(Erase heading not required.)

Army Form C. 2118.

Place	Date	Hour	Summary of Events and Information	Remarks and references to Appendices
ST EMILIE	26th		attack was 3.35 and 27th Apl.	
"	27th	3.55am	The attack was launched 59th Div gaining all objectives, but had to withdraw later from COLOGNE FARM.	DPN
			In conjunction with the attack, 48th Div. pushed out patrols under a barrage arranged by us, endeavouring to advance our outpost line, but finding the enemy in occupation, force and outposts did not advance.	
"	28th		Night firing during nights 27/28 was carried out by A and C/240 on villages and approaches and the Brigade fronts. During the day Onhup fire was carried out with report.	DPN
"	29th		Orders were received that A and D Batteries were to be relieved by two Batteries of 210 Brigade. A and B/211 Batteries were detailed to relieve two Batteries of 210 Brigade. Reliefs were commenced, but section of C/210 relieved a section of A/240, proceeding to hut wagon line at night.	DPN
"	30th		Registration was carried out during the day by the new sections. Colonel Birtwhistle O.C. 210 Bde moved his HQ up to ST EMILIE-115.	DPN

Army Form C. 2118.

WAR DIARY
or
INTELLIGENCE SUMMARY.
(Erase heading not required.)

Instructions regarding War Diaries and Intelligence Summaries are contained in F. S. Regs., Part II. and the Staff Manual respectively. Title pages will be prepared in manuscript.

Place	Date	Hour	Summary of Events and Information	Remarks and references to Appendices
ST EMILIE	30		On the night of 30th 3 guns D/210 were relieved by 2 guns D/210, and one of 210 relieving one section A/240. - The relieved sections proceeding to their wagon Lines.	SPN
			Major B.W. TODD, D.S.O., Lieut F.B. BROOKIBB and 2/Lt. KING PAYNE were struck off the strength of the Brigade during the month, being transferred to England sick. Capt Price and Capt McLeod to joined the Brigade and took command of 3 and A/240 respectively. During the month 26 reinforcements and 55 LD horses were taken on the strength of the Brigade to complete establishments.	SPN

T2134. Wt. W708—776. 500000. 4/15. Sir J. C. & S.

Confidential   Original

240 Bde R.F.A
SR 27

WAR DIARY
of the
240th (SM) Bde. R.F.A

for the period

1st MAY 1917 to 31st MAY 1917

Volume 25.

D.P. Morgan
2/Lt
for LIEUT. COLONEL, R.F.A.
COMMANDING
240th (S.M.) BDE. R.F.A.

Army Form C. 2118.

WAR DIARY
or
INTELLIGENCE SUMMARY.
(Erase heading not required.)

Instructions regarding War Diaries and Intelligence Summaries are contained in F.S. Regs, Part II. and the Staff Manual respectively. Title pages will be prepared in manuscript.

Place	Date	Hour	Summary of Events and Information	Remarks and references to Appendices
	1917			
ST. EMILIE	1st May		During the day relieving sections of 210 Brigade were registered and officers of relieving Batteries were taken round OP's and shewn the country.	D.P.D
"	2nd "	10am	The command passed to O.C. 210 Brigade. 240 Brigade H.Q. moved to Wagon Lines at MARQUAIX relief being completed.	D.P.D
MARQUAIX	3rd "		A and D Batteries still out of the line practised officers and NCOs in laying battery staff work. Backward gunners and drivers received special instruction. B/240 registered barrages for attack on 59th Div. on MARAKOFF FARM. The attack was launched and B/240 fired from 11.30 p.m. to 3.30 a.m.	D.P.D
"	4th "		B/240 fired occasional bursts of fire on MARAKOFF barrage.	D.P.D
"	6th "		Batteries out of the line carried out Gunnery scheme	D.P.D
"	5th "		Batteries out of the line were engaged in tactical exercises. C.O. and O.C. A and D/240 attended G.O.C's conference in the afternoon	D.P.D
"	6th "		Church parade for Batteries out of the line	D.P.D
"	7th "		8 men went on leave. 11 Reinforcements received. B.S.M. PARKER, C/240 transferred to 63 A.Dw. a/R.S.M.	D.P.D

WAR DIARY or INTELLIGENCE SUMMARY.

Army Form C. 2118.

(Erase heading not required.)

Instructions regarding War Diaries and Intelligence Summaries are contained in F.S. Regs., Part II. and the Staff Manual respectively. Title pages will be prepared in manuscript.

Place	Date	Hour	Summary of Events and Information	Remarks and references to Appendices
MARQUAIX	May 1917 8th		A and D batteries went into action to reinforce 42nd Div. Arty.	D.P.D.
			B Battery registered trench near MARROP's FARM and from 9.54 – 10.30 p.m. fired 350 rounds according to programme given them by 42nd D.A. General WARD left 48th D.A. General STRONG took command of 48th Div. Arty.	
	9th		C Battery wagon lines moved from ST. EMILIE to MARQUAIX	D.P.D.
	10th		B Battery wagon line moved to MARQUAIX. One section B/240 came out of action and moved to wagon lines; also one section C/240	D.P.D.
	11th		The second section B/240 and D/240 came out of action and moved to wagon line. Two sections C/240 came out of action and moved to wagon lines; also A/240 Battery	D.P.D.
	12th		B/240 moved remaining section to wagon lines.	D.P.D.
	13		Church parade which all batteries attended. Very heavy thunderstorm on night of 13th/14th.	D.P.D.
	14th		Nothing to report.	D.P.D.
	15th		Orders received for move to new area. C.O. visited Battery positions in new area.	D.P.D.

Army Form C. 2118.

WAR DIARY
or
INTELLIGENCE SUMMARY.
(Erase heading not required.)

Instructions regarding War Diaries and Intelligence Summaries are contained in F. S. Regs., Part II. and the Staff Manual respectively. Title pages will be prepared in manuscript.

Place	Date	Hour	Summary of Events and Information	Remarks and references to Appendices
MARQUAIX	May 16		The Brigade moved off at 6.30 and marching via TINCOURT - TEMPLEUX-LA-FOSSE - MOISLAINS - MANNANCOURT (where the Brigade watered and fed) - MESNIL - ROCQUIGNY - LE TRANSLOY and went into camp near BEAUBENCOURT. about N.11.b.11. (Sheet 57c)	D.P.D
BEAUBENCOURT	17th		Battery Commanders went forward to see their positions. Captains reconnoitred for wagon lines. Orders were received for wagon line to move up on 18th.	D.P.D
"	18th		Batteries moved to their new wagon lines independently in close proximity to VERT WOOD. 2 sections of each battery relieved two sections of 2nd Aust. F.A. Bde. in action in the neighbourhood of HERMIES.	D.P.D
"	19th		Headquarters wagon line moved up to I.36 central. 06. 240 Bde. took command of the Brigade front at 6 p.m. The Bde front extended from K.32.b.0.6 to I.36.b.95. The remaining sections of 240 Bde relieved the remaining sections of 2nd Aust. F.A. Bde during the night. Headquarters 240 Bde were established at I.30.C.6.7 with 145 Inf. Bde. B/240 had one gun damaged	D.P.D

Army Form C. 2118.

WAR DIARY
or
INTELLIGENCE SUMMARY.
(Erase heading not required.)

Place	Date	Hour	Summary of Events and Information	Remarks and references to Appendices
	May 19		Nil chell fire	
BEAUMETZ	20th		(Batteries completed their registration. Lieut-Col the Lord Lynford Lieut M.Hannan and Corpl MILWARD I.H. B/240 mentioned in dispatches. The G.O.C. Division presented the Military Medal to Interpreter HEIN attached 240 Bde R.F.A.	D.P.D
"	21st		During the night 20/21 the Brigade co-operated with 145 by Bns in "crushing" enemy pols K1a 38 and K1a 60. The attack was successful and one prisoner was captured. During the afternoon orders were received that operations concerning the release of gas would be acted on. These orders were subsequently cancelled	D.P.D
"	22nd		D/240 cut wire on the SPOIL HEAP K20 c 67 using 106 fuzes. Operations concerning release of gas were again postponed owing to the wind being unfavourable.	D.P.D
"	23		4.5 How. continued wire cutting on SPOIL HEAP Operations concerning release of gas were again postponed.	D.P.D

Army Form C. 2118.

WAR DIARY
or
INTELLIGENCE SUMMARY.
(Erase heading not required.)

Instructions regarding War Diaries and Intelligence Summaries are contained in F.S. Regs., Part II. and the Staff Manual respectively. Title pages will be prepared in manuscript.

Place	Date	Hour	Summary of Events and Information	Remarks and references to Appendices
BEAUMETZ	May '17 24		D/240 continued wire cutting. Div. Arty. HQ. issued scheme for S.O.S Barrage. D/240 moved one section forward to I.35.a.52 on night 24/25th	D.P.D.
"	25th		D/240 continued wire cutting. During the afternoon BEAUMETZ was very heavily shelled with about 300 15 c.m. D/240 moved another section forward to I.35.a.52 on night of 25/26th	D.P.D.
"	26		D/240 continued wire cutting, and moved remaining section to I.35.a.32	D.P.D.
"	27		Nothing to report	D.P.D.
"	28		Nothing to report the Brigade received reinforcements.	D.P.D.
"	29		Night of 28th/29th A.B. + C. Batteries fired on enemy trenches from 2-3 a.m. in conjunction with discharge of gas and bombardment by T.M. gas shells. Gas was discharged in front of trenches to W. and N. of HAVRINCOURT.	D.P.D.
"	30		C.O. visited the wagon lines	D.P.D.
"	31		Three officers were attached to Anti-Aircraft for instruction in difference of aeroplanes	D.P.D.

Original. Confidential

Vol 2

War Diary
of the
240th (S.M.) Brigade R.F.A.
for the period
1st June 1917 to 30th June 1917.

Volume 27

Army Form C. 2118.

WAR DIARY
or
INTELLIGENCE SUMMARY.
(Erase heading not required.)

Instructions regarding War Diaries and Intelligence Summaries are contained in F. S. Regs., Part II. and the Staff Manual respectively. Title pages will be prepared in manuscript.

Place	Date	Hour	Summary of Events and Information	Remarks and references to Appendices
BEAUMETZ	June 1917 1st.		The Brigade received 9 remounts.	D.P.П.
"	2		During the night 1/2 A, B & C Batteries fired on enemy trenches in front of HARINCOURT in conjunction with a discharge of gas, and bombardment of gas bombs.	D.P.П.
"	3		B Battery were heavily shelled. 2/Lieut L.B Barnes was badly wounded. C/240 one O.R wounded. 2/Lieut L.B Baynes of C/240 was struck off strength on being transferred to England.	D.P.П.
"	4		Nothing to report	D.P.П.
"	5		During the night 4/5th 2 guns B/240 moved forward to J.36.a.9.2. Notification received that Lt Col the Lord Loch Wynyard had been awarded the D.S.O.	D.P.П.
"	6		Night of 5/6 B Battery moved another section forward to J36a 9.2. C Battery heavily shelled, 1 O.R. was wounded. Otherwise no damage. Notification was received that 2/Lieut D.P Morgan, Acting Adjutant had been awarded the M.C. 2/Lieut Barnes who died in hospital on 4th was buried in Military Cemetery	
"	7		at GREVILLERS.	D.P.П.

WAR DIARY
or
INTELLIGENCE SUMMARY.
(Erase heading not required.)

Army Form C. 2118.

Place	Date	Hour	Summary of Events and Information	Remarks and references to Appendices
BEAUMETZ	June 1917 7th		All Batteries of the Brigade co-operated in bombardment of dead ground behind SPOIL HEAP K20a, and bridges over canal and that vicinity. Bombardment of points of fire at irregular hours throughout the day and night.	D.P.D.
"	8th		During the night 7/8th, Batteries co-operated with 145 Bde. in attack on hostile post at K26a95.40. with a view to capturing and establishing a post of our own there. The attack was launched at mid-night and was entirely successful, eleven prisoners were captured. 60CRA held a conference at these Headquarters during the morning.	D.P.D.
"	9"		During the night 8/9 C/240 moved two guns to Wagon Line and 1 gun forward to J36b.2.8 - sniping guns - A/240 moved 1 gun to J35c.0.3. The C.O. held a conference of B.C.'s at forward echange	D.P.D.
"	10th		Liaison with Heavy Artillery started. Major Stirling, Capt. H.P. Lane Lieut. A. J. Rowe and Lieut. J. Brady were attached to	D.P.D.

Army Form C. 2118.

WAR DIARY
or
INTELLIGENCE SUMMARY.
(Erase heading not required.)

Place	Date	Hour	Summary of Events and Information	Remarks and references to Appendices
BEAUMETZ	June 1917 10th		444th H.A.G. and four officers from H.A.G. were attached to the Brigade. Lieut Walworth reported the Brigade H.Q. from 48th Div R.A.H.Q. Batteries bombarded probable H.Q. dugouts in K.15.c.52 and K.21.c. S.S. from 2 – 3.30 p.m. D/240 along B.C.B.R. and S.K. shells. C/240 moved anking gun and one gun from W.br.	D.P.D.
"	11th		[Position] J.11.6.5.8 during the night 9/10th.	D.P.D.
"	12th		Bombardments continued. Barrage not partly returned during the night. #/3 Battery bombarded railway cutting running from K.23.c – K.23.a.	D.P.D.
"	13th		Nothing to report	D.P.D.
"	14th		Lieut Batchelor posted to the C/240 Battery from 48th D.A.C.	D.P.D.
"	15th		Div. O.P. reported large amount of transport on road running N through K.22.a. All Batteries were turned on with very good effect. D/240 moved one howitzer forward to Q.8.c.01.	D.P.D.
"	16th		Arrangements were made to carry out a bombardment of BRIDGE HEAD and trenches in vicinity of U.26 Central. D/240 moved another gun	

T2134. Wt. W708–776. 500000. 4/15. Sir J. C. & S.

Army Form C. 2118.

WAR DIARY
or
INTELLIGENCE SUMMARY.
(Erase heading not required.)

Instructions regarding War Diaries and Intelligence Summaries are contained in F.S. Regs., Part II. and the Staff Manual respectively. Title pages will be prepared in manuscript.

Place	Date	Hour	Summary of Events and Information	Remarks and references to Appendices
BEAUMETZ	June 1917 16th		Forward to Q8C01 to assist in proposed bombardment on bridge head.	D.P.D.
"	17th		Bombardments on BRIDGEHEAD and trenches in vicinity of K12 central, also line of rifle pits at S. of SPOIL HEAP (K20c) were carried out as arranged. 6" howrs and 9.45 T.M's assisting - the former firing 200 rounds, D/240 fired 450 rounds with very good effect.	D.P.D.
"	18th		Bombardments continued. Reconnaissance carried out for placing of three extra batteries for proposed attack on SPOIL HEAP.	D.P.D.
"	19th		Instructions received that attack on SPOIL HEAP will not take place owing to relief of 48th Divisional Artillery.	D.P.D.
"	19th		Orders received that 48th D.A. will be relieved by 23rd — by 13th Aust. F.A. Brigade.	D.P.D.
"	20		The C.O and BC's of 1st Aust. D.A. came up to reconnoitre Battery positions and O.P's preparatory to "taking over".	D.P.D.
"	21		Nothing to report.	D.P.D.
"	22		Two sections per battery of 1st Aust. D.A. relieved two sections per battery of 2nd bde R.F.A. in action. Relief being completed by 1.30 am	D.P.D.
"	23			D.P.D.

Army Form C. 2118.

WAR DIARY
or
INTELLIGENCE SUMMARY.
(Erase heading not required.)

Instructions regarding War Diaries and Intelligence Summaries are contained in F. S. Regs., Part II. and the Staff Manual respectively. Title pages will be prepared in manuscript.

Place	Date	Hour	Summary of Events and Information	Remarks and references to Appendices
BEAUMETZ	June 1917 23rd		Registration of relieving sectors completed by 12 noon.	D.P.D.
		6 p.m.	The command passed to 2nd Cavl. Bde, 1st Cavl. B.A. Remaining sectors were relieved after dusk, and 2nd Bde proceeded to its wagon lines at VERT WOOD	
MONTAUBAN	24		2nd Bde marched to camp just S. of MONTAUBAN via LE BŒUFRE, FREMICOURT, BAPAUME, LEBARS, POZIERES LA BOISELLE, CONTALMAISON BAZANTIN LE GRAND arriving in camp about 4 p.m. The G.O.C. Division inspected the Bde on the line of march, and complimented the Brigade on its turn out. All guns requiring overhaul were left at I.O.M. No.2 workshop at BAPAUME.	D.P.D.
"	25		The Brigade proceeded to overhaul all stores and equipment and refit.	D.P.D.
"	26		Nothing to report.	D.P.D.
"	27		28 Remounts were received.	D.P.D.
"	28		Nothing to report	D.P.D.
"	29		Nothing to report	D.P.D.
"	30		Nothing to report.	D.P.D.

CONFIDENTIAL.   ORIGINAL

WAR DIARY

OF THE

240ᵀᴴ (S.M.) BRIGADE, R.F.A.

FOR THE PERIOD

1ˢᵀ to 31ˢᵀ October 1917

Volume 31.

D.P. Nixon
Capt. Adjutant
p/. LIEUT. COLONEL, R.F.A.
COMMANDING
240th (S.M.) BDE. R.F.A.

Headquarters,
    48th Div. Arty.

Herewith original copy of WAR DIARY of the 240th (S.M.) Brigade, R.F.A., Volume 31, for the period 1st October to 31st October, 1917.

D.P. Morgan
Capt. & Adjutant,
240th (S.M.) Brigade, R.F.A.

1/11/17

WAR DIARY
INTELLIGENCE SUMMARY

Army Form C. 2118.

Place	Date	Hour	Summary of Events and Information	Remarks and references to Appendices
October 1917				
OCHTEZEELE	1st		Bde out at rest	DPM
	2nd		Lt. Col. C.M.C. Rudkin returned from leave took command of Brigade.	DPM
	3rd		Nothing to report	DPM
	4th		do	DPM
WATTOU	5th		Brigade moved to WATTOU area via WINNEZEELE and went into camp for the night.	DPM
	6th		Personnel of Bde R.F.A. in action 240 r. & OR's were entrained 50" Bde R.F.A. in action 240 r. 241 Bdes were entrained to form No 3 Sub. Group RA under Lt. Col Rudkin. H.Q.rs were established in the Ramparts at YPRES	DPM
YPRES	7th		Nothing to report.	DPM
	8th		All day practice barrages. 7.O.O.'s reconnoitred forward O.P.s	D.P.M
	9th		Btys cooperated in attack - which was partially successful D.P.M. Group H.Q. moved forward to HUSSAR FARM. Lt. Bde W.C. moved forward to the outskirts of YPRES. 21 Lt. 70 ORS S.K. Afro wounded	D.P.M

Army Form C. 2118.

WAR DIARY
or
INTELLIGENCE SUMMARY.
(Erase heading not required.)

Instructions regarding War Diaries and Intelligence Summaries are contained in F. S. Regs., Part II. and the Staff Manual respectively. Title pages will be prepared in manuscript.

Place	Date	Hour	Summary of Events and Information	Remarks and references to Appendices
	October 1917			
YPRES	10"		Btyn reported S.O.S. lines. C/120 had 1 O.R. killed + 1 O.R. missing	DPM
	11"		Nothing to report.	DPD
	12"		Btyn co-operated in an attack at dawn - own reinforcements were held in readiness for an advance. This attack was only partially successful	DPM
	13"		Bde came out of action remained at W.Ls for the night.	DPD
EECKE	14"		The Bde marched to EECKE via Switch Road, POPERINGHE - ABEELE and billetted there for the night	DPD
MORBECQUE	15"		March continued via HAZEBROUCK to MORBECQUE	DPD
GONNEHEM	16"		March continued via ST.VENNANT + ROBECQ to GONNEHEM after leaving MORBECQUE the Bde came under command of the First Army.	DPM
ABLAIN-ST-NAZAIRE	17"		BC's proceeded by lorry to reconnoitre BGs from the taken over from 5" Bde C.F.A. The B'DE marched to ABLAIN-ST-NAZAIRE via CHOQUES - NOEUX-LES-MINES present in conv.	DPM

WAR DIARY
or
INTELLIGENCE SUMMARY.
(Erase heading not required.)

Army Form C. 2118.

Place	Date	Hour	Summary of Events and Information	Remarks and references to Appendices
	October 1917			
ABLAIN-ST. NAZAIRE	18th		Two sections of A, B, & D/240 relieved 2 sections of S' Bde C.F.A. in action. C/240 remaining out of action at their W.T.S.	D.P.N.
VIMY.	19th		Remaining sections of A, B, & D/240 relieved remaining sections of S'Bde C.F.A. Lt. Col. Rudkin taking over command of group on completion of relief. 20" Bty. C.A.F.A. attd. to group in place of C/240. A, B, D/240 & 20 Bty C.A.F.A. comprising Rt Group. 4 & 5 Div Arty. HQrs established in VIMY ridge	D.P.N
"	20th		All Btys checked registration. A, B, & D Btys handed over guns to replace guns taken over from S'Bde C.F.A. in action. Positions for each Bty in the Group were reconnoitred.	
"	21st		Sniping sections for each Bty in the Group were reconnoitred by Btys C.O.s. S.O.S. at 7:30 am. All Btys fired - Enemy did not attack. During night section of D/240 & 20"Bty C.A.F.A. occupied sniping positions.	D.P.N.
"	22nd		New S.O.S. lines arranged. also MUTUAL SUPPORT & Rt Half. During night A & B/240 moved sections to sniping positions.	D.P.N
"	23rd		S.O.S. at 5:30 am. Enemy did not attack.	D.P.N.

WAR DIARY
or
INTELLIGENCE SUMMARY.
(Erase heading not required.)

Army Form C. 2118.

Place	Date	Hour	Summary of Events and Information	Remarks and references to Appendices
VIMY.	October 1917 24th	—	C/240 relieved 24" Bty C.A.P.A. in action taking over guns & stores in situ. 24" Bty C.A.P.A. proceeded to W/L where they were under orders from their own Brigade	DPN
	25"		A/240 moved to another position close by. L.O.E. & R.A. inspected A + B By positions. A+B Bty I.O.R. wounded. A Bty during action heavily shelled.	DPN
	26		Nothing to report. 90 L.D. evacuated to M.V.S. for details.	DPN
	27"		L.O.E. R.A. & Bde visited A, B, C Btys. Arrangements made for removal of Horse HQ to THELUS CAVE to join Hvy Bde H.Q. 69 L.D. mules recd.	DPN
THELUS.	28"		Bde H.Q. moved to join Hvy Bde at THELUS CAVE.	DPN
	29"		Nothing to report.	DPN
	30"		E.O. helped scheme for raid on hostile enemy post at about T.10 b 83. This was subsequently cancelled owing to patrols having discovered the post was not held at night.	DPN
	31"		D.D.V.S. V Corps inspected sick lines of the Bde. Bde formed a special sick line for eye cases.	DPN

www.ingramcontent.com/pod-product-compliance
Lightning Source LLC
Chambersburg PA
CBHW081526160426
43191CB00011B/1695